Latina Activists across Borders

Latina Activists across Borders

Women's Grassroots Organizing

in Mexico and Texas

MILAGROS PEÑA

DUKE UNIVERSITY PRESS ∿ DURHAM & LONDON 2007

10/8/01

$18.55

4BP

In memory of my mother,

MILAGROS AMPARO MARTÍNEZ LÓPEZ,

and grandmother GRACIELA MARÍA TEJADA MAÑÓN,

whose lives inspired me to fight for women's rights.

This book is also dedicated to my husband,

FRED HAMANN, *who has never faltered*

in encouraging me to pursue my dreams.

Contents

Acknowledgments

The research for this book was supported by a 1995 Fulbright Hays/García Robles research grant and a faculty research grant from New Mexico State University, Las Cruces. I am also deeply indebted to Maruja González Butrón and others of the Equipo de Mujeres en Acción Solidaria (EMAS) in Morelia, Michoacán, for inviting me to begin my research at EMAS. Maruja's generous reception and the doors she opened to women's organizations in Michoacán and elsewhere in Mexico made this research possible. The Centro Mujeres de Fe y Esperanza of El Paso, Texas, the first site I visited in greater El Paso/Ciudad Juárez, also opened its doors and gave me access to its networks. Without the Centro, the southwest part of this study would not have been possible. Colleagues and friends at New Mexico State University, Las Cruces, and the University of Florida encouraged the project, provided critique, and extended friendships that kept me going during the research and writing of the book. At New Mexico State University, Las Cruces, I want to thank Christine Eber, Lisa Frehill, Lisa Lucero, and Bill Walker. At the University of Florida, I thank Paula Ambroso, Kendal Broad, Connie Shehan, and Danaya Wright. My family, in particular my husband, Fred Hamann, and my sister, Jane Nuñez, are the reason I can find the inspiration, support, and love I need to pursue my research. I especially thank them for providing me with the time away from them to pursue this book project. Finally, I would like to thank the women in Michoacán and El Paso/Ciudad Juárez who shared their stories and visions for the women's organizations that appear in this book. This book is a testimony to the courage and leadership they bring to the women's movement.

Nongovernmental Organizations Studied

Annunciation House of El Paso, Texas
Asociación Ayuda Mutua, Morelia, Michoacán
Asociación de Pastoras, Mexico City
Asociación Ecologista Viva Natura, Uruapán, Michoacán

Battered Women's Shelter, El Paso, Texas
Bienestar Familiar, El Paso, Texas

Centro de Apoyo a la Salud Alternativa (CASA), Morelia, Michoacán
Centro de Atención a la Mujer Violentada (CAMVI), Morelia, Michoacán
Centro de Estudios Sociales y Ecológicos (CESE), Pátzcuaro, Michoacán
Centro de Servicios Municipales Heriberto Jara (CESEM), Morelia,
    Michoacán
Centro Mujeres de Fe y Esperanza, Ciudad Juárez, Chihuahua
Centro Mujeres de Fe y Esperanza, El Paso, Texas
Centro Mujeres Tonantzín, Ciudad Juárez, Chihuahua
Centro para el Desarrollo Integral de la Mujer, A.C. (CEDIMAC), Ciudad
    Juárez, Chihuahua

Equipo de Mujeres en Acción Solidaria (EMAS), Morelia, Michoacán
Equipo de Promoción a la Salud Comunitaria (EPROSCO), Morelia,
    Michoacán

Grupo Civil de Mujeres Gertrudis Bocanegra, Pátzcuaro, Michoacán

La Mujer Obrera, El Paso, Texas
La Posada, El Paso, Texas

Michoacanos Unidos por la Salud y contra el Sida, A.C. (MUSSAC),
Morelia, Michoacán

Mujeres de Nocutzepo, Pátzcuaro, Michoacán

Mujeres del Magisterio Democrático, Morelia, Michoacán

Mujeres Grupo Erandi de Pichátaro (Mujeres de la Nación Purépecha),
Morelia, Michoacán

Mujeres por la Democracia, Pátzcuaro, Michoacán

Mujeres Unidas, Anthony, New Mexico/Texas

Organización Popular Independiente (OPI), Ciudad Juárez, Chihuahua

Taller Permanente de Estudios de la Mujer de la Escuela de Mujeres de la
Universidad Michoacana, San Nicolás de Hidalgo, Morelia, Michoacán

VenSeremos, Morelia, Michoacán

Women's Intercultural Center, Anthony, New Mexico/Texas

Young Women's Christian Association (YWCA), El Paso, Texas

Interviews with Leaders

of Nongovernmental Organizations

Alvarez Ugena, Elena. Asociación Ecologista Viva Natura, Uruapán, Michoacán, July 23, 1995.

Berresheim, Ida. Centro Mujeres de Fe y Esperanza, El Paso, Texas, April 22, 1998.

Buchmueller, Florence. YWCA, El Paso, Texas, June 1, 1999.

CASA group interview. Morelia, Michoacán, June 28, 1995.

Cira Gómez, Yadira. Taller Permanente de Estudios de la Mujer de la Escuela de Mujeres de la Universidad Michoacana San Nicolás de Hidalgo, Morelia, Michoacán, May 12, 1995.

Combs, Rosemary. Battered Women's Shelter, El Paso, Texas, July 7, 1999.

Concha, Eleonor Aida. MPD, Mexico City, March 20, 1995.

Cortez, Dulce. Mujeres por la Democracia, Pátzcuaro, Michoacán, June 27, 1995.

Erickson, Kathleen. Women's Intercultural Center, Anthony, New Mexico/Texas, May 25, 1999.

Flores, María Antonia. Mujer Obrera, El Paso, Texas, May 26, 1999.

García, Imelda. Bienestar Familiar, El Paso, Texas, June 9, 1999.

García, Rubén. Annunciation House, El Paso, Texas, June 9, 1999.

González Butrón, Maruja. EMAS, Morelia, Michoacán, April 1, 1995.

Graciela [pseudonym], El Paso, Texas, February 26, 1996.

Gringas Aguirre, María de Jesús. Centro Mujeres Tonantzín, Ciudad Juárez, Chihuahua, June 10, 1999.

Guadalupe, Carmona. Grupo Civil de Mujeres / Mujeres Gertrudis Bocanegra, Pátzcuaro, Michoacán, July 13, 1995.

Habur, Bernadette. La Posada, El Paso, Texas, May 12, 1999.

Kustusch, Donna, and Eleanor Stech. Centro Mujeres de Fe y Esperanza, Ciudad Juárez, Chihuahua, June 7, 1999.

Leony, Dolores. CEDIMAC, Ciudad Juárez, Chihuahua, June 14, 1999.

Lozano, Itziar. Red entre Mujeres, Mexico City, February 15, 1995.

Mejía, María Consuelo. Católicas por el Derecho a Decidir, Mexico City, February 17, 1995.

Monreal Molina, Patricia. OPI, Ciudad Juárez, Chihuahua, June 10, 1999.

Montoya, Francisca, independent activist, and Diana Bustamante, Colonias Development Council of Doña Ana County, New Mexico, Phoenix, Arizona, March 22, 1997.

Mujeres de Nocutzepo group interview. Pátzcuaro, Michoacán, May 9, 1995.

Navarro, Fernanda. VenSeremos, Morelia, Michoacán, May 19, 1995.

Pineda, Yolanda. MUSSAC, Morelia, Michoacán, January 28, 1995.

Sandoval, Tomasa. Mujeres de la Nación Purépecha, Morelia, Michoacán, June 1995.

Sansón, Chela. Mujeres del Magisterio Democrático, Morelia, Michoacán, May 18, 1995.

Santamaría Galván, Ana. Asociación Ayuda Mutua, Morelia, Michoacán, April 28, 1995.

Suárez, Consuelo. CESE, Pátzcuaro, Michoacán, May 24, 1995.

Suárez, Rocío. CIDHAL, Cuernavaca, Morelos, May 3, 1995.

Tamez, Alma. Asociación de Pastoras, Mexico City, June 21, 1995.

Torres, Concepción ("Coni"). CESEM, Morelia, Michoacán, May 22, 1995.

Villalobos, Delia. EPROSCO, Morelia, Michoacán, May 8, 1995.

Mexican and Mexican American Women's Activism

in NGOs: Background on the Michoacán and

El Paso/Ciudad Juárez Communities

Some time ago a friend told me about an exchange she had witnessed at a women's forum in El Salvador. The meeting brought together women from different socioeconomic, educational, ethnic, and racial backgrounds to discuss a host of women's issues and plans for action. At the meeting the word *feminismo* was used by women active in feminist circles. On the last day of the meeting a woman stood up and asked if someone could clarify for her the word's exact meaning. She asked if it meant "fe-en-mi-mismo," literally "faith in myself." If so, she added, then she believed in it.

My friend's story left a lasting impression on me, because it highlighted Latinas'[1] more general struggle with what *feminism* means and with what kind of feminism we embrace in our activism. In fact, feminist activist researchers in gender and development studies have lamented that "outside of academia, within policy and activist arenas, the utility and relevance of 'gender' has been highly contested"; further, they argue, "'gender' has come to lose its feminist political content," in particular in grassroots circles (Baden and Goetz 1997: 37). I disagree. This book highlights how grassroots women process their situations and inform themselves and each other about mobilization strategies. Some do so in nongovernmental organizations (NGOs), developing gender consciousness through their activist work, often opting for goals in line with global feminism.[2] Sonia Alvarez (1997: 94) notes that empowering women requires "a flexible, multidimensional feminist strategy—one that organizes gender-conscious political pressure *at the base*, both within and without the state."[3] It is a strategy adopted by NGOs in Michoacán and in the greater metropolitan area of El Paso, Texas, and Ciudad Juárez, Chihuahua, and it is a focus of this book. By studying women's NGOs in these communities we do not simply uncover Mexican and Mexican American grassroots contributions to women's activism; we also better understand the goals grassroots women embrace as they fight for women's rights.

Because this book is itself a feminist project, I used a feminist research approach of oral history and conversation. This allowed me to connect as a Dominican American with Mexican and Mexican American women. While aware that I was not Mexican, Mexican American, or Chicana, as a child of Latin American immigrants, I knew I shared a history and cultural heritage that linked me to the women who participated in this study. We spoke the same language, though our intonations were different. Our stories included family struggles to make ends meet while working multiple shifts in low-paying jobs. We grew up in a society where the voices of Latinas/os, whether documented or undocumented, mattered little. And as women, we found it more difficult to have a meaningful voice in families and societies that often consign us to the margins. Once our conversations began, our backgrounds drew us closer. The connections allowed me to foster a trust that opened doors, so that I could ask questions that often an outsider cannot without raising suspicions. In my case, being an insider was important. I felt comfortable talking about feminism and did not worry that someone might get offended or challenge the use of the word. For a great majority of the women in the NGOs I discuss here, the issues we share as Latinas connect us fundamentally and bring us to women's organizations. Therefore, throughout the book I recognize the particular voices and contributions of Mexican and Mexican American activists without essentializing their experiences, recognizing that their particular struggles echo those of other Latina communities. Consequently, I refer to *Latinas* wherever the echoes of this term highlight broader implications for Mexican and Mexican American women's activism. Looking at the larger context of how women's NGOs in Michoacán and El Paso/Ciudad Juárez came into existence underscores the importance of and potential in understanding why and how particular social contexts shape women's activism.

Throughout the project I was challenged by grassroots women's activism, as I believe others of my generation have been. As this book will show, grassroots women engage in and seek alliances and coalitions in mainstream feminist spaces where not too long ago they felt and perhaps still feel underrepresented or not represented at all. In this book, grassroots Mexican and Mexican American women activists allow all of us to look at how we can break barriers and work across women's activist communities. However, I am aware that "the appeal to coalitional politics" can undermine feminist politics, as Sally Baden and Anne Marie Goetz (1997: 53) correctly warn. These tensions emerge throughout this book, such as in chapter 4, which examines the limits of women's activism in these structures. Despite these limits and potential pitfalls, we can learn much from women's activism in NGOs, which is breaking new ground, allowing us to envision the benefits of global feminist approaches, particularly in the growth of women's NGOs as part of an evolving "global feminism."

Because of my transnational, U.S.-Mexico focus, 1995 and the UN Fourth World Conference on Women in Beijing provided a rich historical moment. The events leading up to the conference allowed me to study a cross section of the women's movements in international, transnational, and local contexts. Women's NGOs in Michoacán participated extensively in preparatory meetings for the Beijing conference; those in El Paso/Ciudad Juárez did less so. Francisca Montoya, an activist who has worked on the U.S.-Mexico border since her college days, described the benefits of networking for and going to Beijing:

> For the women that went to Beijing you had the opportunity to meet women from other countries. You had an opportunity not only to share what you're doing, but the work that you're doing and who you are and what you're about and what you're hoping to accomplish. . . . but at the same time during the process we were able to listen to what other

women were doing. It's such a unique opportunity [not only] to come back . . . energized about who you are and what you're doing but . . . to be around other women, to get ideas.

Despite the benefits some saw in the networking and the efforts leading up to the Beijing conference, not all women's activist communities engaged fully in the preparations or in the meeting itself. This book explores why some women's communities participated more extensively than others in the Beijing process. Much of the answer lies in events impacting women's activist communities and in the strategies with which the groups respond to such events. María de Jesús Gringas Aguirre, cofounder of Centro Mujeres Tonantzín in Ciudad Juárez, noted that while her organization was part of the local committee organizing for Beijing, much of the local activism in El Paso/Ciudad Juárez focused on the murders of border women in the Juárez desert. They put their energies into marches highlighting violence against women and more generally showing the border to be an economically and politically exploited community.

These differences in activist strategies can be important to students of social movements who are interested in whether extensive resources or large networks are necessary for successful social activism. As I hope to show, sometimes movement success is not so straightforward. Women's NGO successes and failures cannot be measured by their ability to mobilize resources and networks. In looking at the activism of Mexican and Mexican American women, we see that they mobilize and articulate their needs within specific sociohistorical realities. When we understand how women's NGOs emerged in their social contexts, we see that grassroots women have taken the personal and made it political, which in itself can be a measure of success, given that for some it is the first step toward self-empowerment. In an interview for this book, Dulce Cortez, cofounder of Mujeres por la Democracia (Women for Democracy) in Pátzcuaro, Michoacán, stated:

One of the things important to me in this work is gaining knowledge in order to share it with the other women I represent in this area. I have come to see that for me the most important thing is for our society to take us into account. I work to overcome the fact that we have been socialized to take care of children and husbands. Our group has become politically involved to show that we exist and to have our political parties take us into account.

For Cortez and others I interviewed for the book, Mexican and Mexican American women's sphere of influence in public domains compels us to see personal lives as public struggles for justice. Women's NGOs highlight this point in stating their goals, and the theme permeates documents prepared for the Beijing conference.

Therefore the conference and meetings leading up to it help us to understand women's activism and the issues it raises locally and globally. Of particular interest is how local, national, and international political realities either create or limit social movement opportunities. Focusing on the sociopolitical context of different women's activist communities also allows us to understand why one community engages more extensively than others in expansive networks. The comparison in this book of two women's activist communities with similar cultural heritages and colonial realities is perfect for addressing the limits and opportunities in women's NGO activism. But by no means do I suggest in this comparison that Mexican and Mexican American women's identities or histories and political realities are the same. But in many ways Mexican and U.S.-Mexico border communities share a historical and political tapestry framed in U.S.-Mexico socioeconomic relations. Therefore in trying to understand border-crossing activism, whether in Mexico or on the U.S.-Mexico border, I look to build on several notions that the Chicana feminist and cultural theorist Gloria Anzaldúa (1999: 84) left us before she died in 2004: "Nosotros los Chicanos [We the Chicanos] straddle the borderlands. . . . Deep in our hearts we believe that being Mexican has nothing to do with which country one lives in. Being Mexican is a state of soul — not one of mind, not one of citizenship, neither animal respects borders." Mexican and Mexican American communities share much, particularly in their religious cultures, woven from indigenous and Spanish colonial legacies. But one of the most pervasive and potent cultural symbols that binds Mexican and Mexican American communities is La Virgen de Guadalupe: "Guadalupe unites people of different races, religions, languages" (ibid.: 52). This is why, notwithstanding Patricia Zavella's (1997: 185–94) note of caution in recognizing the diversity among Mexicans and

Mexican Americans, Anzaldúa also contributed greatly to our understanding of common grounds. Also, some, like the sociologist Pablo Vila (2000), correctly note tensions among people of Mexican ancestry in how they perceive each other across the U.S.-Mexico political divide. However, these tensions are less evident in border women's NGOs, which are working across many border communities (Staudt 1997; Staudt and Coronado 2002). This book is a testimony to the spaces that women's NGOs create for women to dialogue and work across geographical, class, race, and gender boundaries.

I follow Anzaldúa's recommendation and view Mexican and Mexican American histories as a framework for understanding women's activism and sociopolitics. Hence my focus on the border-crossing metaphor. The women of Michoacán and the women of greater El Paso/Ciudad Juárez, feeling the impact of an increasingly globalized capitalism, have become aware that women's border communities share much in common. Discussing her research for the La Mujer Obrera (the Woman Worker) organization of El Paso, Sharon Navarro (2002: 189–90) noted that "La Mujer Obrera's mobilization of its women members to appeal to U.S. city, state, and federal institutions has been largely grounded in the creative use of elements of Mexican culture and attempts to build transnational cultural bridges across the border." In Mexico and the U.S. Southwest, global capitalism has made such bridges essential.

GLOBAL CAPITALISM AND THE GROWTH OF WOMEN'S NGOS

Saskia Sassen (1998) argues that the infrastructure of capitalism is now strategic, precise, and focused on enabling private corporations and financial, cultural, consumer, and labor markets to operate internationally. Because of the growing need for NGOs to respond to the effects of this globalization, it is important to understand their histories and recent growth in this context. To do so I begin with the observation that NGOs are diverse institutions having two things in common: they are separate from any state or government agency and they engage in social work or community organizing around social issues (Talamante Díaz, Careaga Pérez, and Parada Ampudia 1994: 327). Typically, they are described as social service institutions, doing social good and promoting economic and social development, whether they are part of social movements or not. In recent years, NGOs have flourished, "expanding [the] public policy agenda, both confronting and nudging at governments, international development organizations, and the people that staff bureaucracies in those institutions" (Staudt 1997: vii). In answering why NGOs have flourished and their policy agendas have expanded, the political scientist Kathleen Staudt noted, "The Fourth World Conference on Women, under United Nations auspices, is one important reason among many. Actually several UN-affiliated international meetings in the early 1990s established strong connections to women and gender-fair agendas, including those on the environment (1992), human rights (1993), social development (1995) and most importantly, populations and development, held in Cairo (1994). Beijing, however, was a threshold" (vii).

More specific to Latin America and the origins of some NGOs working in the U.S. Southwest are three historically significant events: (1) the 1960s U.S. economic plan for Latin America called the Alliance for Progress, followed more recently by the neoliberal policies of the North American Free Trade Agreement (NAFTA); (2) the Catholic Church's Second Vatican Council, which encouraged religious organizations to work more closely with the poor; and, (3) the church's Latin American Episcopal Conference in Medellín, Colombia, in 1968, which also emphasized working with poor and marginalized groups (Rubén et al. 1991; Staudt 1997; Sassen 1998; Staudt and Coronado 2002).

In the wake of these events, one notes two basic types of NGOs: those that channel resources and administer projects funded and shaped by the strategies of organizations like the U.S. Agency for International Development (U.S. AID), and those that are supported by nongovernmental actors like philanthropic foundations and are more committed to grassroots organizations (Rubén et al. 1991: 60–61). These more "nongovernmental" NGOs, which are more likely to have evolved from protest or resistance groups, are the ones that tend to link themselves to and become part of women's movements. As I will show, women's NGOs can deepen the women's agenda by mobilizing with global economic and political perspectives. How extensively mobilizing occurs is a related and an important question that, I argue, is best understood in the local histories of feminist and other movements.

To date there is no official record of the total number of women's NGOs in

Mexico or the U.S. Southwest. But research does show that the rise there of NGOs focused on women's issues is a recent phenomenon. From 1986 to 1991 there were eighty-six registered organizations in Mexico that worked specifically "to better women's social conditions" (Martínez 1991). Of these 70 percent were established in Mexico City. Twenty-five percent were founded after 1970, most after the 1980s, with the greatest increase in the 1990s. Alicia Martínez (1991: 9–10) found that, of the women's organizations registered in Mexico, 52 percent were listed as NGOs, 14 percent were associated with universities, 10.5 percent were governmental organizations, and 22 percent were distributed among varying types of private institutions, including churches, with the remaining 1 percent not specified. Mexican organizations focused on gender from 1970 to 1991 emphasized specialized services for women in the areas of health, legislation, and help for victims of sexual and intrafamily violence.

No comparable study of women's NGOs exists for the U.S. Southwest. The research has looked at women's activism on the U.S.-Mexico border, with an emphasis on the link between border human rights issues and women's issues. The human rights focus entails emphasis on cross-border collaborations: "Activists in the human rights arena are constantly struggling to promote their agenda on both sides of the border because human rights issues transcend the border" (Staudt and Coronado 2002: 135). U.S.-Mexico border activists tend to stress issues related to immigration, labor exploitation, the disappeared, and violence against women. But as the interviews for this book show, even women's border issues transcend their localism. The human rights issues articulated at the U.S.-Mexico border resonate deep within Mexico and raise some of the core human rights issues articulated at the Beijing conference. Consequently, while I focus on Mexican and Mexican American women's NGOs, I find two important patterns that apply to the activism of Latinas and third world women more generally: (1) the recent emergence of NGOs focused specifically on women's issues and (2) the stress that women's activism in Mexico and the U.S.-Mexico border communities places on affiliations across ethnicity, race, and class, often leading these struggles for women's and human rights to encompass other issues, including environmental ones, as Claudia Sadowski-Smith (2002) notes. Despite differences in mobilizing strategies, women's groups in Michoacán and in El Paso/Ciudad Juárez are strikingly similar. The two communities highlight new directions in women's activism. But to understand these women's communities, we must first examine the particular historical events that inform their activist strategies. Doing so sheds light on how two distinct women's communities speak to activist strategies generally and Latina activism specifically, as well as on their visions of global feminist futures. The following is a brief historical background of the two women's communities I study in this book.

BACKGROUND ON THE WOMEN'S MOVEMENT IN MEXICO

Before 1980, feminist organizations in Mexico found it difficult to make inroads with women of the grassroots or, as some put it, popular sector (Espinosa Damián and Sánchez Olvera 1992: 17). During the late 1960s to 1970s only a limited feminist discourse circulated among grassroots women's groups. Early in the Mexican women's movement, a distance separated grassroots women from, for lack of a better word, academic feminism. Women I interviewed for this book noted that Mexican feminists in the 1960s and 1970s were middle- to upper-class academics who spent little time working with grassroots women. In the 1980s all that changed. At the Primer Encuentro Nacional de Mujeres (First National Women's Gathering) in Mexico City in 1980 Mexican feminists discovered the differences between their interests and those of women of the popular sector, and they were challenged by the dialogue with them (ibid.: 18). The Encuentro was the first meeting where the women's groups represented cut across class lines. It lasted three months and attracted around five hundred women, most representing poor urban barrios.

According to the Mexican feminist historians Gisela Espinosa Damián and Alma Rosa Sánchez Olvera (1992), those in attendance generally came from independent popular organizations such as the Frente Popular Tierra y Libertad (Land and Liberty Popular Front) of Monterrey, a number of *comunidades eclesiales de base* (base Christian communities, or CEBS),[4] and women from the "10 de abril" community in the state of Morelos. Representatives from greater Mexico City included the residents of Ixtapalapa and Netzahualcóyotl, as well as of the *colonias* of Guerrero, Ajusco, and Cerro del Judío. Rural communities were represented by a peasant movement that was quite visible at the time, including the community of Venustiano Carranza in the state of Chiapas, as well as communities in Veracruz, Aquila, and Michoacán. Also present were union organizers and representatives of other NGOs, including militant women from the Nicaraguan Frente Sandinista de Liberación Nacional (Sandinista National Liberation Front) and from a number of Salvadoran and Guatemalan grassroots organizations. According to Espinosa Damián and Sánchez Olvera (1992), among the NGOs central to the planning and technical support for the Encuentro were Comunicación, Intercambio y Desarrollo Humano en América Latina (Communication, Exchange, and Human Development in Latin America, or CIDHAL) and Mujeres para el Diálogo (Women for Dialogue, or MPD).

Consequently, the Mexico City conference was the first to represent the grassroots mobilization that has characterized the present-day women's movement in Mexico. The diversity of this gathering and subsequent Encuentros forced women's groups in Mexico to think and mobilize across class and racial lines. Since then grassroots women's NGOs have proliferated. Lorenia Parada Ampudia's analysis of a 1992 directory of women's NGOs identified eighty-eight that worked with grassroots women's groups (Talamante Díaz, Careaga Pérez, and Parada Ampudia 1994: 5). Of those, forty-seven (53 percent) were located in Mexico City, the rest being distributed throughout fourteen states. The same analysis showed that eighteen (20 percent) of these NGOs were founded before 1981, twenty-two (25 percent) between 1981 and 1985, thirty-three (37 percent) between 1986 and 1990, and eight (9 percent) between 1991 and 1992 (a small number reported no founding dates). Parada Ampudia's findings show that after the 1980 Encuentro the Mexican women's movement increased its ties with grassroots sectors. Also significant was the number of the NGOs springing up outside Mexico City, a decentralization that would be critical to women activists working in Mexican states that traditionally receive little attention from the central government.

Cecilia Talamante Díaz, Gloria Careaga Pérez, and Lorenia Parada Ampudia (1994: 339) identified five themes guiding the objectives of Mexican women's NGOs: (1) fortification of women's organizations, (2) changing women's conditions at work and in the home, (3) defending victims of gender violence, (4) promoting better health conditions, and (5) addressing class issues of inequality. Health concerns related to reproductive health and violence. They also show that the NGOs primarily worked with women from peasant, indigenous, and colonia communities. How the Michoacán women's NGOs worked, how they linked class and race issues to gender issues, and to what extent they were linked to other grassroots groups (not focused on gender) were questions posed in this study. Women's NGOs in Michoacán and their networks became increasingly visible during preparations for the Beijing conference.

THE BEIJING PREPARATIONS

Approximately twenty women's NGOs in Michoacán mobilized in the "Toward Beijing" efforts. Listed below, they were founded between 1983 and 1993, with a majority after the late 1980s. A June 1995 general assembly report, found in the Equipo de Mujeres en Acción Solidaria (Team of Women Solidary in Action, or EMAS) archives, noted that it was not until the Michoacán State Coordinating Committee formed to prepare for Beijing that local network organizing heightened (Minutes 1995). The report highlighted activities that the committee supported, including International Women's Day, the Campaign for Children's Day, and the Day of Action for Women's Health, to mention a few of the activities designed to lead women's local groups to collaborate and network with each other.

The Michoacán State Coordinating Committee became important for its role on several other panels. It developed ties to the Central Region Organizing Committee and to other networks that linked the Michoacán board to Mexico's national "Toward Beijing Leading Committee." The latter was important because it facilitated access to prominent actors in the national women's movement, providing opportunities for alliance with their NGOs. The "Toward Beijing Leading Committee," for example, consisted of figures including Itziar Lozano of Red entre Mujeres (Network among Women), Lorenia Parada Ampudia of the Programa Universitario sobre Estudios de Género (University Gender Studies Program, or PUEG), Patricia Duarte of the Colectivo de Lucha contra la Violencia hacia las Mujeres, A.C. (Fight against Violence toward Women Collective Inc., or COVAC), Lucero González of the Sociedad Mexicana pro-Derechos de la Mujer (Mexican Society for Women's Rights), and Cecilia Loría of the Grupo de Educación Popular con Mujeres (Group for Popular Education with Women, or GEM). Access to members of the "Toward Beijing Leading Committee" was crucial because they met with other groups in Latin America and the Caribbean to advance issues important to Mexican women.

As part of the preparations, the UN's "Toward Beijing" organizers had divided Latin America into five regions: (1) the Andean countries, (2) Brazil, (3) Central America, (4) Mexico, and (5) the Caribbean. For its part, Mexico's Central Region Organizing Committee brought state NGO committees into preparations for Beijing. The state committees were organized by region, linking Michoacán with other states in central Mexico (Aguascalientes, Colima, Guanajuato, Hidalgo, Jalisco, Morelos, Puebla, Querétaro, and San Luis Potosí). A report, titled *Hacia la IV Conferencia mundial sobre la mujer en Pekín (hoy Beijing)*, or *Toward the Fourth World Conference on Women in Peking (Today Beijing)*, published by the Central Region Organizing Committee, revealed an extensive network that became important to the women's groups in Michoacán (Coordinadora de la Region Centro 1994).

This book explores how the "Toward Beijing" networking efforts opened up grassroots mobilizing opportunities locally, nationally, and transnationally. Social movement theorists stress the importance of networking, which "open[s] up access to participation" (Kriesi et al. 1995: 53). Networking also makes groups and individuals aware of "the availability of influential allies" (ibid.), creating or enhancing political opportunities and giving participants "a good sense of the important advantages of block mobilization of activists" (Zald 1992: 334). The experience of Tomasa Sandoval, an indigenous leader I interviewed from the Purépecha Nation of Michoacán, illustrates this point well. Sandoval became active in the women's movement during the "Toward Beijing" process. The network opportunities enhanced indigenous women's causes locally and brought them closer to the larger women's movement. Sandoval was pivotal to the process as a leader and spokesperson of Mujeres Grupo Erandi de Pichátaro (Erandi Women's

Group of Pichátaro), one of two Purépecha women's NGOs that participated in the "Toward Beijing" efforts in Michoacán. Sandoval also linked local women's groups to the broader Purépecha Nation, in which she also was a leader. The opportunities for exchange with local indigenous communities made local NGOs more aware of the plight of indigenous people throughout Mexican society, as events in Chiapas, with its indigenous insurrections, have underscored.

The political struggles for indigenous recognition in Michoacán and throughout Mexico have a long history. Indigenous people's fight for land and against political and economic marginalization parallels much of the history of Mexico's peasantry more generally (Velázquez 1992). However, differences between indigenous struggles and those of the broader peasantry emerge when we consider the system of class and gender domination, which has produced a particular type of marginalization for indigenous people since the colonial period. The system of race, gender, and class domination has exposed indigenous women to triple jeopardy. Margarita Velázquez (1992: 48–49) argues that indigenous men, although marginalized by race and class, have been able to establish limited relationships with the larger Mexican mestizo society, but indigenous women have not. Even when government policy toward Mexico's indigenous people began to change (1920–40), indigenous women were "confined to their communities, without possibilities of any major contact with mestizo society" (ibid.: 49). Velázquez argues this essentially gave indigenous women no access to an indigenous educational politics. During the 1970s, this politics would be challenged by an indigenous movement that itself would be challenged by indigenous women. I discuss this point further in chapter 1.

Suffice it to say here that Tomasa Sandoval's leadership in the Michoacán women's NGO and Purépecha Nation networks brought her to national prominence, as she would be named "national coordinator for indigenous women." Her leadership and the presence of indigenous women's NGOs like Mujeres Grupo Erandi de Pichátaro would be symbolic of the growing diversity of the women's movement in Mexico.

While Michoacán women's NGOs reached out beyond the state capital, Morelia, to surrounding towns, as well as state, national, and international organizations, women's NGOs in greater El Paso/Ciudad Juárez networked much more locally. Why the difference? Is it less crucial than what the two communities can teach us about grassroots women's organizing more generally? The more local focus in El Paso/Ciudad Juárez was not necessarily a limitation. What this book shows is that success in women's mobilization should not be measured primarily in terms of ability to mobilize material resources or move in vast networks. While these are significant, I argue that for many marginalized people success lies more in moving women to action in public and private spheres. In other words, while forming organizations to fight labor exploitation, homelessness, and broader political exclusion is important, empowering women to fight domestic violence and to gain a sense of themselves as people with a voice outside and within the home is just as important. As the women I interviewed express, the path from personal to broader women's issues is often the road to women-centered activism.

One could argue, as I do here, that the differences between NGO mobilization in El Paso/Ciudad Juárez and in Michoacán result from the specific histories that tie the women's organizations to their sociopolitical contexts. The mobilization of Chicanas and Mexican American and Mexican women in El Paso/Ciudad Juárez is linked to the history of local movements and to the current politics of the U.S. southwestern borderlands.[5] In other words, just as women in Michoacán have had to face off against the particular class and racial histories of Mexico, women of Mexican descent on the U.S.-Mexico border have had to gain their voice in the context of class and racial politics particular to that region. Imelda García of Bienestar Familiar in El Paso related an exchange with a woman she was helping to confront domestic violence; it underscores what the undocumented on the U.S.-Mexico border have to overcome: "When you're dealing with issues of domestic violence, you learn what I learned as I talked to a woman the other day[:] . . . you need to establish something that won't scare us when we call." Some of the women who come to the NGOs are undocumented workers; some fear dishonoring their families if they talk about them publicly. As García testified, border women's NGOs struggle to help women overcome the feeling that they have to carry the burden of domestic violence to protect the men in their families, whom they sometimes see also as victims because they are unemployed or face racism. NGOs on the border have to empower people in a social context where fear undergirds labor exploitation with racism and sexism. On the U.S.-Mexico border fear takes on other meanings for the uprooted, undocumented, and un- or under-employed.

The League of United Latin American Citizens (LULAC)[6] and the Chicano movement were born in this border reality. But throughout the history of even these political responses to marginalization, one thing has remained constant: the particular status of border women and their fight for political empowerment. In organizations like LULAC that fight for the political rights of peoples of Mexican and, more broadly, Latin American descent in the region, women have had to fight for their place. Belén B. Robles, who ran unsuccessfully for president of LULAC in 1970, noted that "women of Hispanic ancestry or Spanish descent have perhaps a harder time in obtaining equal opportunities because of the machismo that prevails among the Hispanic."[7] Recalling her 1970 defeat, Robles commented that LULAC members "weren't quite ready to have a woman as a national president despite the majority seeing her as the best qualified." Robles was elected president in 1994 and served four consecutive one-year terms.

Prior to Robles's presidency, leadership by the women of LULAC was largely in community organizing and grassroots activism. Mary Lou Armendariz, a member of Ladies LULAC Council 9 of El Paso recalled that much of the council's work centered on preparing people to become citizens and raising money to help underprivileged children.[8] Armendariz and others in the ladies council also became active in election campaigns. In 1957 they supported Raymond Telles for mayor of El Paso. In fact, much of LULAC's work in El Paso during this period consisted of promoting Latinos for public office or civic engagement through social works. But by the early to mid-1960s, these strategies proved ineffective for young Latinos, who saw organizations like LULAC as too mainstream. Many young Latinos joined the new Chicano movement, in which leaders like Reies López Tijerina argued for a land grant, an effort to force the U.S. government to honor its

1848 Treaty of Guadalupe Hidalgo with Mexico. Rodolfo (Corky) Gonzales and others founded the Crusade for Justice. The farmworkers' movement took hold under the leadership of César Chávez and Dolores Huerta. And La Raza Unida came to life in Crystal City, Texas, as a third party fighting inequities in the political power structure of Texas and other states where significant numbers of Mexicans and Mexican Americans lived but few held political office.

In "El Movimiento" (the Chicano movement), according to Alma García (1989, 1997), women of Mexican descent gained a new political voice. They critiqued their traditional gender roles in the romanticized Mexican family by demanding a greater leadership role in the Chicano movement. Mexican American women identified as Chicanas to underscore their borderland roots and to challenge the patriarchal culture that cast them as homemakers whose primary responsibility was caring for their children and husbands (Zavella 1987; Segura 1991). These issues came to a head as women in Chicano organizations were relegated to sexist traditional gender roles, where men spoke and women listened or did secretarial tasks. The Chicano movement drew out Chicana feminists as women fought to end sexist oppression within a broader nationalist effort to end racist oppression (Alma García 1989: 220). But in the end, the Chicano movement allowed little room to address the status of women inside and outside the Chicano or Mexican border community. Chicanas saw themselves as triply oppressed because of their race, class, and sex; those who took feminist stances often were accused by Chicanos of being race traitors. Chicanos charged that Chicana feminists were influenced by an ideology from the white mainstream. Chicanos labeled Chicana feminists as "malinchistas," or traitors to the Mexican race. The reference is to Malinche, the indigenous woman who became the translator to Hernán Cortés, the Spanish conqueror of Mexico. In this version of history, Malinche facilitated Mexico's conquest. As Anzaldúa (1999: 5) noted, for many, Malinche, or Malintzín, became "the fallen Eve who 'betrayed' her people." Anzaldúa and other Chicana feminists rejected this version of history, noting that "the Aztec nation fell not because *malinali* (La Malinche or La Chingada) interpreted for and slept with Cortés, but because the ruling elite [within Mexico at the time] had subverted the solidarity between men and women and between noble and commoner" (56). These and other challenges to Mexican and U.S. interpretations of women's history were highlighted by Mexican, Mexican American, and Chicana feminists to show how such ideologies subordinate women. These tensions and historical developments underscore why Latinas created their own political spaces in Mexico, on the U.S.-Mexico border, and elsewhere.

In a piece titled "The Woman of La Raza," Enriqueta Longauex y Vásquez, a columnist and cofounder of the New Mexico–based Chicana newspaper *El Grito del Norte*, noted the painful reasons why women's organizations are necessary.

> What usually happens to this woman [Mexican women who challenge their communities] when she tries to become active in the *"Causa?"* [the Chicano cause]. One would think that the movement would provide a place for her. One would think that the organizations would welcome her with open arms and try to encourage her to speak up for her *Raza* [race]. One would think that because of her knowledge and situation the groups would think of liberation schools with child care for the victims of broken homes, in order to teach them culture and history so that they may find self-identity. When she tries to speak of *machismo*, she is immediately put down. . . . She receives nothing but censorship again. She tries so much to speak up and instead finds herself speaking to deaf ears and completely closed minds. (Longauex y Vásquez n.d.)

Women have responded to this marginalization by creating their own political spaces, shaping their organizations to meet a number of objectives, the first of which is to empower their members.

Mexican and Mexican American women who form their own NGOs tend to reject hierarchical forms of governance. In describing the organizational structure of La Mujer Obrera (the Woman Worker) in El Paso, its director, María Antonia Flores, noted: "We do not have a pyramid. We have a collective organization, an organization that functions through a collective working, with respect, and collective unity. Yes, within it we have a board of directors as any organizations needs, . . . but the implementation of our work is a circular one as a collective, as equals." Other goals for women's NGOs include forming alliances and coalitions with other groups to maximize efforts, outreach, and solidarity.

Some argue that alliances and coalitions are facilitated on the U.S.-Mexico border because "members of [borderlands] diasporas exhibit multiple loyalties, move between regions, and often become themselves conduits for the increased flow of money, goods, information, images, and ideas across national boundaries" (Sadowski-Smith 2002: 3). As Anzaldúa (1999) noted, the borderland is a place where several cultures, histories, and people's experiences meet and shape politics. In addition, the border's sociopolitical and economic context itself motivates women in El Paso and Ciudad Juárez to seek each other out and organize across class and ethnic boundaries. Undeniably, U.S.-Mexico border experiences draw women into activism, and women's NGOs downplay differences between Mexican and Mexican American border women. In fact, Mexican scholar María Socorro Tabuenca Córdoba (1995–96: 154) criticizes the figurative use of the border as "a multicultural space in the United States," arguing that this promotes a narrow view of Chicana/o identities (see also Sadowski-Smith 2002: 2). The U.S.-Mexico border is instead a region that has drawn Chicana/o as well as other Mexican and Mexican American activists into the broader political realm in which border NGOs operate.

Consequently, for many interviewed in this book, *Chicana/o*, rather than being a term for defining oneself as part of a borderlands history different from Mexican, is a marker of their political coming of age in the Chicano movement. Imelda García of the Centro Mujeres de Fe y Esperanza (Faith and Hope Women's Center) of El Paso noted that she came to the women's movement and ultimately to border community work as part of an awakening to the fight for border justice. Her experiences in the Chicano and Chicana movements raised questions for her as she was trying to find her place as a Mexican American in the U.S. women's movement.

I got involved with a women's group at the university [Sul Ross State University in Alpine, Texas]. And I struggled with it, because we had a lot of differences. I think being right out of the Movimiento Chicano, I could see a lot of differences in the way that we saw issues, because in the

Movimiento Chicano, even though we women were pushing and pushing ahead, we saw "a esos hermanos" [those brothers]. We were both
being treated wrongfully. You know, treated badly. And so it was very
difficult, because we didn't consider them the enemy, and for the wom-
en's movement a lot of times the men were the enemy.

García underscores the layering of her activist trajectory, including why
mainstream U.S. feminism is limiting for border women. But García's dis
connect with mainstream U.S. feminism is part of a larger story. Her experience illustrates why Latina organizations tend to see themselves as part of a
"women's" movement rather than a "feminist" one.

This tension is best captured in the observation by the Chicana feminist
Martha Cotera (1977: 36) that "all White women 'herstory' publications
have been severely criticized for being blatant in their disregard for the
pluralistic aspects of our society." For many women of color, feminist organizations in the United States promote "white" women's feminism and are not
for them. Not surprisingly, a similar disconnect also exists in Mexico, this
time between grassroots (particularly indigenous) women and upper-class
mestiza (lighter-skinned Spanish-Indian) women. Consequently, wom-
en's narratives in this book underscore areas where academic feminists have
failed to speak to grassroots women, and so the term *feminist* often is
rejected.

Yet the historical disconnects I identify, with all the challenges they
pose, have not deterred Latinas from creating new spaces for women's
activism. Latinas and non-Latinas on both sides of the U.S.-Mexico border
—whether indigenous, mestiza, white, or academic feminists—are engaged
in an activism that has made possible new feminist or women-centered
visions. NGOs have become spaces for women to connect, share their experiences, raise gender consciousness, and develop networks that offer myriad
opportunities for social activism. Social and personal crises bring women to
NGOs "to network, to interact, and to communicate" on issues central to
their needs and from there to "influence, negotiate, and make decisions"
that empower them as a group (Melucci 1995: 45). Moving from personal
crises, which often begin in local communities, to activism can be an important process in the development of a political voice.

The political scientist Carol Hardy-Fanta (1993: 18–19) suggests that grassroots politics, as locally based community organizing, is characteristic of the Latina mobilization she observed in Boston; but her analysis highlights a more general pattern in Latina activism: "With their emphasis on grassroots politics, survival politics, the politics of everyday life, and the development of a political consciousness, Latina women articulate connections between the problems they face personally and the issues they face as part of their ethnic communities stemming from government policies [and other practices that marginalize women]." Consequently, women-focused NGOs create and nurture spaces where the personal and political awaken not only gender consciousness but also commitment to social activism, and where coalitions and alliances can be forged through organizing. The latter is a feature of Mexican and Mexican American women's mobilization in Michoacán and in greater El Paso/Ciudad Juárez.

Alliances and coalitions can be formed with groups that may seem unlikely allies. A unique contribution of this book to the study of women's organizing is its look (in chapter 3) at alliances with women's religious organizations. Of note are the contributions of Catholic sisters who are organizing with grassroots women in Mexico and on the U.S.-Mexico border. Some Catholic sisters engage in social activism because Catholic Church policy since the mid-1960s has promoted community work in poor and marginalized communities. Inspired by these changes in policy, women's Catholic religious communities revisited their organizational missions and embraced community work that includes working with women's activist organizations. Some interviewed for this book also noted the influence on them of the Brazilian educator Paolo Freire, who promoted empowering models for working in marginalized communities. Others were inspired by liberation theology and the challenge women brought to it. One of the untold stories in the history of liberation theology in Latin America is the challenge women posed to liberation theologians and the Catholic Church on the question of women's status in society. This also is often left out of discussions of the history of the women's movement in Latin America and in the United States. As I briefly note below, the connection between women's grassroots NGOs and faith-based women's organizations is central to understanding the breadth and depth of women's activism in Mexico and on the U.S.-Mexico border.

BRIDGING THE SECULAR AND THE RELIGIOUS: THE RELIGIOUS
CONNECTION TO GRASSROOTS WOMEN'S ORGANIZING

To understand the engagement of Catholic sisters in grassroots women's community work and NGOs, we must consider background events that to some may seem irrelevant. Why did they work for women's causes in grassroots communities in Mexico and on the U.S.-Mexico border? Part of the answer lies in the emergence of liberation theology and subsequent debates in the Catholic Church. Ultimately, women's organizations found liberation theology to have limited benefits for women, and women's faith-based organizations embraced women-centered activism. When liberation theology emerged in 1968 at the Latin American [Catholic] Bishops' Conference in Medellín, Colombia, advocates attacked social and economic injustice and the institutions that promote inequality. From Medellín on, liberation theology came to mean solidarity with the poor as a fundamental religious and ethical concern quite different from any position the Catholic or other church had taken in the past. According to a number of liberation theologians, the struggle for the liberation of the oppressed in society required new economic and political strategies to narrow the enormous gap between rich and poor in Latin America and throughout the third world (Silva Gotay 1981). Liberation theologians were known for supporting poor people's movements, recognizing that social change could only come through political activism. But liberation theologians mostly focused on class inequality and on economic and political policies as its root causes. They paid no specific attention to how inequality is exacerbated by gender effects, an omission challenged by feminist theologians and women's groups.

In pushing liberation theology to focus on gender in the 1970s, women's religious organizations called into question patriarchal religious authority and associated social institutions that conspire to marginalize women. As I discuss in chapter 3, women's religious groups, some led by Catholic sisters, banded together with grassroots women's organizations to mobilize against patriarchy and the social institutions that promote it. For both religious and nonreligious women and feminist activists, collective identities are tied to a general goal or theme articulated in women's liberation struggles wherever they manifest themselves. The collective gender-based identities and political articulations in this book highlight the overlap among women's experiences of marginalization and the visions for liberation they share, whether faith-based or not. As I argue in chapter 3, the history of faith-based organizations, such as those discussed in this study, is important to understanding women's activism in larger women's movements. Latina theologians underscore this point in their writings, identifying several reasons for it.

María Pilar Aquino's (1992) book *Nuestro clamor por la vida*, on Latin American theology from the perspective of women, outlines several factors that link the economic, political, and social realities of Latinas in the United States and in Latin America. Aquino analyzes women's experience of both class and gender oppression. In Latino communities where a majority is baptized Roman Catholic, the Catholic colonial legacy continues to play an important role in undermining the position of Latinas in the home, in their communities, and in their churches. Patriarchy here is understood as part of a legacy that conspired against women, as Catholicism not only condoned but advocated granting exclusive rights to men in building on Spanish pre- and postconquest communities. Thus, regardless of Latinas' geographical origins, they share a common Spanish colonial cultural heritage that makes their experience more similar than distinct when it comes to the social institutions they engage in their daily lives. This is why I use the term *Latina* to focus on women's experiences that extend beyond Mexico and the U.S.-Mexico border. Moreover, the kind of transnational bridge-building done by women's NGOs in Mexico and the U.S. Southwest has become increasingly necessary with the advent of global capitalism. The cross-border linkages among Mexican and Mexican American women activists that will be shown in this book help us understand how global feminisms evolve. Of course, Mexicans and Mexican Americans are diverse and do argue among themselves, as writers such as Patricia Zavella (1987) and Pablo Vila (2000) have shown. But the El Paso region is perhaps the most Mexican of U.S. border communities. According to the 2000 U.S. census, 78 percent of El

Paso residents reported being of "Hispanic" origin (as the U.S. Census Bureau refers to peoples of Spanish and Latin American descent), with 66 percent identifying as Mexican; 71 percent reported speaking Spanish at home; and 27.4 percent reported being foreign-born (U.S. Census Bureau 2000). Furthermore, Irasema Coronado, Sharon Navarro, and Kathleen Staudt, among other authors whose works I cite in this book, show that NGOs here are engaged in cross-border activism identified with U.S.-Mexico border justice issues. These issues include but are not limited to labor, homelessness, racism, and violence. They have particular consequences for women in their day-to-day lives.

For low-income Latinas, Aquino (1992: 20) argues, daily life is marked by the oppression of a patriarchal *machista* system inherited from Iberian colonialism, the present imperialist-capitalist forms of which subject them to subordination, racial prejudice, increasing poverty, and systematic exclusion on the sole basis of their gender. According to Chandra Talpade Mohanty (2003: 144), that legacy has expanded to a patriarchal dominance and women's exploitation in "the development and operation of a 'new' world order. . . . Third World women workers (defined in this context as both women from the geographical Third World and immigrant and indigenous women of color in the United States and Western Europe) occupy a specific social location in the international division of labor that illuminates and explains crucial features of the capitalist processes of exploitation and domination." These are the forces that bring Latinas together and that motivate us to challenge dominance that controls us in our homes and in society at large. And while men's status and their complicity to promote institutions of privilege can vary by class and race, patriarchy bestows on all men rights over women. Under this system, men rule at home and it is up to women to protect the "honor of the family." As Rosa Linda Fregoso (2003: 18) notes, in this context "violence against women and sexual assault are typified in law as crimes against the honor of the family, rather than as crimes against the personal, physical integrity and human rights of the woman victim." Fregoso suggests that such views reinforce "a discourse that discourages women from leaving the private sphere, the purported site of patriarchal protection and authority: public space is imagined as inherently dangerous" (ibid.). Men, in contrast, regardless of their own class- or race-based marginalization, can appeal to the patriarchal privileges that at least give them power over women. Still, it is true that poor people's movements can create opportunities for race-, class-, and gender-based alliances, though these are often framed as separate struggles, with good reason. The Chicano movement offers one example of how alliances are used. Fighting against the social institutions that have marginalized women does not always mean rejecting them and beginning anew.

Instead, women subvert first their family roles, then their roles in the community, sometimes beginning in their churches. Latina activism in base Christian communities is often cited as an example of how women challenge traditional spaces, transforming them into sites for community activism where women are empowered. Susan Eckstein (1999: 8) notes that "Base Communities have been a force behind a range of movements." Aquino (1992, 19) adds that "today's popular social movements and the different base Christian communities recognize the role of women everywhere in their community." Research on these base Christian communities shows that community projects have had two basic goals: day-to-day survival and the democratic participation of their members in interpersonal relations, in the group's struggle against authoritarianism, and in its relationships with other grassroots organizations (Montes 1987: 83). These grassroots groups seek to confront hunger and poverty and to strengthen popular organizations by incorporating women. Consequently, I focus on pastoral and community work that is linked to women's activism. To ignore this broader dimension of Latina religious practice, that is, its mobilization in community or pastoral work, would be to misunderstand the complex ways in which Latinas become agents of social change and what they bring to feminism and larger women's movements.

COALITIONS, ALLIANCES, AND WOMEN'S ORGANIZING

The research I conducted in Mexico and on the U.S.-Mexico border shows that Latinas define themselves as women in public spheres that engage a broad spectrum of women's activism across ethnic, class, and religious boundaries. I contend that Latina activism advances women's issues, claiming myriad identities while at the same time furthering the interests of larger

Latina/o communities. Looking at Latinas and the cultural context in which they operate helps us understand why women work in women's NGOs that also engage broader community issues. The sociologist Mary Pardo (1998a: 228), who studied the Los Angeles neighborhoods of Boyle Heights and Monterey Park, noted that "in both communities, women's activism originated in family concerns and community networks, then generated broader political involvements." More significant is Pardo's observation that "within the circumstances of [Latina's] lives, they use existing gender, ethnic, and community identities to accomplish larger political tasks" (ibid.). These larger political missions are often responses to political or economic contexts that marginalized communities, and women in particular, face in a changing global economic context.

Having organizations that can draw women to act against such forces is critical to improving women's lives globally. Developing strategies to confront the forces of global capitalism is no easy task, and it requires collaboration among like-minded people. Women in the two communities I studied identified core issues that their NGOs address, including the marginalization of women by a patriarchal system of dominance; violence against women; the increasing number of single women who head households and raise families while under- or unemployed; abuse of low-income workers that affects women in particular ways; and health, environmental, and other issues that link women to larger human-rights concerns.

To confront the global political and economic forces that women face, women's NGOs recognize the potential political benefit of coalitions and alliances. I see an important distinction between these two forms of association. As Papusa Molina (1990: 329) notes, *coalitions* are about "achieving goals as the main objective, but [they are] often characterized by temporary strategizing." When objectives are achieved, coalitions often disband. This is sometimes a useful strategy, as it was for women's NGOs preparing for the Beijing conference. But alliances have greater potential: formed around commitments to individuals, they bring together organizations with a shared vision of how society can be improved, a vision sustained throughout the duration of a movement and among networks of committed activists.

Where appropriate I also use the terms *women-centered movement* and *women's movement* because, as Muruja González Butrón of Equipo Mujeres en Acción Solidaria (EMAS) of Morelia noted, "the term *feminist* for grassroots women is something little understood." As the vignette with which I opened this introduction reveals, it is a term that circulates primarily among academic women and that when used in NGOs is rarely understood and is sometimes seen as divisive. There is the sense that *feminism* means something radical, separatist, and different from other women's desire for an inclusive liberation of the oppressed in their society. Outside feminist circles, feminism is seen as excluding and bashing men, with no real meaning for the day-to-day experiences of grassroots women. These women also feel that marginalized men stand to gain from a women's liberation movement (as opposed to a feminist one that bashes men). Therefore, in studying women's NGOs in Mexico and the U.S. Southwest, I examined the contributions of women activists as they articulated their political activism in practices and visions for an inclusive global feminism.

THE RESEARCH PROJECT

My comparative analysis of Latina women's NGO activism in Michoacán and greater El Paso/Ciudad Juárez showed me how mobilization patterns can differ even between communities that share a culture and history. More important, the research illuminated the social context in which Latinas mobilize in NGOs as part of our participation in larger women's movements — in my view, consistent with global feminism.

In oral history interviews, I began by asking eighteen basic questions focusing on organizational history: how the leader of the organization got involved in the women's movement; the organization's goals; and its financial sustainability, publications, outreach, and networks. In feminist research (Behar and Gordon 1995; Reinharz 1992), oral histories allow participants in a study to reflect on their experiences, what they believe, how they came to build their organizations, and how those beliefs have impacted their everyday lives and those of their fellow activists. It was with these intentions that I approached my interviews. Using a "snowball sample," continuing until I no longer found new NGOs mentioned in interviews, I identified sixteen organizations within the network cluster in Michoacán. I began this sampling with the Equipo de Mujeres en Acción Solidaria because EMAS was an organization mentioned in the literature as having network ties to Mujeres para el Diálogo (Women for Dialogue, or MPD), the organization that challenged the Latin American Bishops' Conference in Puebla, Mexico, in 1979, as I discuss in chapter 3. EMAS also met my criteria of a faith-based women's organization in a larger women's movement, one in which its leader and cofounder, González Butrón, was a central figure. My interview with her led me to other women leaders and to the EMAS archives, where I found the names of other women's NGOs in Michoacán. From January 1995 to July 1995, I interviewed twenty leaders of women's NGOs, primarily in Michoacán. The four interviews in Mexico City included women leaders who helped me document historical events and understand ties to NGO leaders in Michoacán.

The Michoacán NGOs included, in Morelia, the Asociación de Ayuda Mutua (Mutual Aid Association), the Centro de Apoyo a la Salud Alternativa (Center for Support of Alternative Health, or CASA), the Centro de Atención a la Mujer Violentada (Center for Women Victims of Violence, or CAMVI), the Centro de Servicios Municipales Heriberto Jara (Heriberto Jara Municipal Services Center, or CESEM), the Equipo de Promoción a la Salud Comunitaria (Promotion Team for Community Health, or EPROSCO), EMAS, Michoacanos Unidos por la Salud y contra el Sida, A.C. (Michoacanos United for Health and against AIDS, Inc., or MUSSAC), Mujeres del Magisterio Democrático (Women for Democratic Teaching), Mujeres Grupo Erandi de Pichátaro (also known as the Mujeres de la Nación Purépecha), the Taller Permanente de Estudios de la Mujer de la Escuela de Mujeres de la Universidad Michoacana, San Nicolás de Hidalgo (Permanent Research Group for Women's Studies at the Women's Program of Michoacán University, San Nicolás de Hidalgo), and VenSeremos (whose name can be understood as either "We Will Win" or "Come and We Will Be"); in Nocutzepo, Mujeres de Nocutzepo; in Pátzcuaro, the Centro de Estudios Sociales y Ecológicos (Center for Social and Ecological Studies, or CESE), the Grupo Civil de Mujeres Gertrudis Bocanegra (Gertrudis Bocanegra Civil Women's Group), and Mujeres por la Democracia (Women for Democracy); and, in Uruapán, the Asociación Ecologista Viva Natura (Live Nature Ecological Association). The four women interviewed in

Mexico City were Eleonor Aida Concha of MPD, Itziar Lozano of Red entre Mujeres; María Consuelo Mejía of Católicas por el Derecho a Decidir (Catholic Women for the Right to Choose), and Alma Tamez of the Asociación de Pastoras (Association of Women Pastors).

Using the same snowball sample technique, I identified thirteen NGOs in greater El Paso/Ciudad Juárez. For similar comparison to the Michoacán organizations, I chose the Centro Mujeres de Fe y Esperanza in El Paso to begin this half of the study. I began in El Paso because I was working at New Mexico State University at the time and the Centro was a women's faith-based NGO in the United States similar to EMAS with a membership composed predominantly of Chicanas, Mexicans, and Mexican Americans, that is, one with the same cultural and historical heritage as women in Mexico. In particular, I was looking for communities to compare across borders, because, as sociologist Valentine Moghadam (2000) argues, transnational feminist networks have become increasingly important for women's collective action in the era of globalization. It also became clear as my study progressed that the Centro was the women's organization most mentioned by other women's groups in El Paso/Ciudad Juárez as one with which their NGOs shared programs, personnel, and events. This indicates the Centro's pivotal regional role, similar to that of EMAS in Michoacán.

From the thirteen NGOs identified in the greater El Paso/Ciudad Juárez area, sixteen leaders were interviewed. Two Chicanas who have worked in the Southwest with women's groups and other activist organizations were included because they helped clarify historical events in the region. In total, the study that is the basis for this book included thirty-nine interviews. Those in greater El Paso/Ciudad Juárez were conducted from spring 1998 to summer 1999. The El Paso/Ciudad Juárez women's NGOs included, in El Paso, Annunciation House, the Battered Women's Shelter, Bienestar Familiar (Family Well-Being), La Mujer Obrera, the Centro Mujeres de Fe y Esperanza, La Posada (The Inn), and the YWCA; in Ciudad Juárez, the Centro Mujeres Tonantzín (Tonantzín Women's Center), the Centro para el Desarrollo Integral de la Mujer, A.C. (Center for the Complete Development of Women Inc., or CEDIMAC), the Centro Mujeres de Fe y Esperanza, and the Organización Popular Independiente (Popular Independent

Organization, or OPI); and, in Anthony, Texas/New Mexico, the Women's Intercultural Center and Mujeres Unidas (Women United).

As chapter 2 will show, a distinguishing feature of women's organizing in El Paso/Ciudad Juárez is their locally based mobilization strategies. Historical reasons for these dynamics are discussed further in chapter 2. Diana Bustamante, executive director of the Colonias Development Council of Doña Ana County, New Mexico, shared her thoughts on border mobilization strategies: "One of the phenomena of the Southwest is that we're immediate—working on a day-to-day survival basis." Bustamante noted that border issues come with specific demands. Francisca Montoya, who also has years of experience in community work in the Southwest believed that border cities, even large ones like El Paso (pop. 564,000), tend to organize almost exclusively at the neighborhood level.

These and other factors are important to understand, because one could get the impression that women's NGOs in Michoacán are more effective, given the extent of their networks and given their mobilization beyond the local level. I caution readers to reserve judgment until the end of the book. Political activism at any level can be daunting. People organize for social change and adopt strategies that make practical sense and maximize efforts. My own thinking was challenged by a plaque that hung on the wall of one of the women's NGOs I visited as I began this research. It read: "Think globally, act locally." Borrowed from the international environmental movement, the slogan reflects some of the women's thinking: no matter how small the effort, we are fighting for women's rights globally when we engage in our own local communities.

This book offers insight into how women working together can be effective even if efforts remain local. Grassroots women in this book offer their organizing stories as part of their view of struggles that bring women together to fight for social justice. As Tomasa Sandoval of Michoacán noted, "We are participating because we believe that the only way that we can really move ahead as women is to be united and organized to fight for gaining [political] space as women." María of El Paso said, "[My] own experiences with family violence connected me to fight for broader women's issues, because family violence has devastated me."[9] She now works in NGOs in

El Paso and Ciudad Juárez to help women gain a sense of themselves and their rights. These and other narratives throughout the book underscore grassroots women's call for global and transnational strategies that empower them to action. In looking at two Latina communities in a transnational context, we better understand women's mobilization, how they become agents of social change, and how they are shaping our feminist future.

CHAPTER ONE

Women's Activism in Michoacán

Understanding the emergence of an NGO in any part of the world requires looking at the economic, political, and historical forces that gave rise to it. In the next two chapters, I lay the foundation for understanding why and how women's NGOs in Michoacán and El Paso/Ciudad Juárez became important to women's mobilization in these two communities. The discussion shows that women's mobilization is marked by responses to sociopolitical marginality rooted both in larger community struggles and in activists' particular experiences as women in those struggles.

According to a 1990 study conducted by the Mexican Consejo Nacional de Población (National Population Council, or CONAPO) cited and analyzed in a Team of Women in Solidary Action, or EMAS, report entitled *Las mujeres en Michoacán, Junio 1994*, Michoacán is among the states with the highest degree of marginalization (EMAS 1994). The report analyzed data such as the literacy rate for Michoacanos older than sixteen (17.32 percent), the percentage of the over-sixteen population that had not completed elementary school (48.56 percent), and the percentage of households without a drainage system, electricity, or potable water (58.46 percent). In comparing these data by sex, the study found women's literacy rates to be even lower than men's. Women's dropout rates from elementary and high school were greater, which can be attributed to the expectation for women to fill domestic roles, particularly caring for children.

Of Michoacanos employed outside the home, women were 19.83 percent, while men were 80.17 percent. Significant in this last comparison is the fact that only 39 percent of Michoacanos over twelve are employed. Women working outside the home are concentrated in domestic or "pink" collar occupations, such as domestic work, office support, factory work, and teaching and other jobs related to education. In sum, their work outside the home is concentrated in occupations that are an extension of work women are expected to do in the home. The data published in *Las mujeres en Michoacán*, compiled by the economist and EMAS cofounder Maruja González Butrón, show that when women work, they receive lower wages than men, face sexual harassment, and, because most are poor, work double and triple shifts, endangering their physical and mental health.

On the political front, while women have been very involved in organizing the fight for democracy and the right to vote in Mexico, few are elected or appointed to positions of power (EMAS 1994). The reason given is usually women's low levels of education. Women's NGOs like EMAS note that patriarchal structures impede women's educational progress. The marginalization of Mexican women in the home is reproduced outside it, particularly in the workplace and political sphere. In Michoacán's capital, Morelia, only one of the twenty state agencies is headed by a woman. In the state legislature, only one of the seventeen state deputies is a woman. Of the state's judges, fifty-seven are men and fourteen are women. And of the five judicial positions considered to be the second and third most important, one is held by a woman.

The dismal picture painted in the CONAPO research analyzed by EMAS helps us understand the emergence and proliferation of women's NGOs in Michoacán. But only partly, because, as I will argue throughout this book, and as other research on social movements has shown (McAdam and Snow 1997), marginalization, though an important ingredient in mobilization, does not explain mobilization by itself. Leadership, committed activists, resources (including other movement networks), and propitious historical moments are also critical. The experience of EMAS shows much of what is needed not only to mobilize potential supporters but also to awaken in them the consciousness necessary for a community of protest.

In *Las mujeres en Michoacán*, EMAS recommended that the first step to mobilizing women be strengthening their work in and with other women's organizations that have overlapping interests. Networking could be done through gatherings or conferences, including cosponsored workshops, where all the organizations committed themselves to sharing ideas and exchanging resources in a women's network. "The connections and complimentary potential [in networking] signify STRENGTH" (EMAS 1994). Building this network strength in Michoacán began with the efforts of EMAS. As we look at Michoacán's women's networks, we also find that networking plays an important role in forming leaders. It is no accident that one of EMAS's cofounders, González Butrón, was the author of the report and brought mobilizing savvy to the Michoacán women's communities. Her background in EMAS and her connections to other women's groups in Mexico prior to founding EMAS show that movement leadership is nurtured in many social movement locations. In other words, women with previous experience in other movement organizations, whether these groups are feminist or not, often emerge as leaders.

IN THE BEGINNING: MOBILIZING OUT OF CRISIS

The early history of EMAS, established in Mexico City in 1985 and now based in Morelia, is typical of women's NGOs; it also shows how women like González Butrón facilitated mobilizing across social movement networks in Mexico in the 1980s. That is, they were connected both to specific community service organizations serving women in the popular sector and to social movements. The contacts and community work strategies of movement participants help to mobilize resources for their communities because the activists can promote the projects of both larger marginalized communities and women in particular. In a 1995 interview, González Butrón recalled:

Our group began working around March of 1985. We were women who had come from other experiences with other women's groups who shared similar work objectives and perspectives. Most of us were working in *colonias populares* above all because important things had been accomplished there. We were very much interested in the problems of women from the colonias populares. There was at the time [early to mid-1980s] the Coordinadora Nacional del Movimiento Urbano Popu-

lar [National Coordinating Committee of the Urban Popular Movement, or CONAMUP]. This was a very important space because it
grouped the principal independent organizations of the colonias populares at the national level. And women had, with a lot of effort and after
much debate, created their own space there. This effort began in Mexico
City and was called the Regional de Mujeres del Valle de Mexico [Wom-
en's Regional Committee of the Valley of Mexico] of the CONAMUP. . . .
We believed that united we could provide service.[1]

In the year EMAS was founded, 1985, a powerful earthquake hit Mexico
City, a crisis to which NGOs of all kinds were called to respond. This spurred
women's grassroots organizing in Mexico City and later throughout the
country, causing women's organizations to proliferate in the 1990s. Not
only did NGOs discover the level of network activism at their disposal and its
power, but all the mobilization around helping the victims of the earthquake solidified some organizations and gave birth to many others. The
proliferation of women's NGOs in Mexico can be traced to the 1985 earthquake crisis. González Butrón recalled the disaster's impact:

> During that whole process of the urban popular movement a terrible
> event occurred in Mexico precisely the year that EMAS emerged, which
> was the earthquakes of September of that year. And really the situation in
> Mexico City was grave at the time and it was precisely in the center of the
> city where the worst damage hit. At the time, we were doing some work
> with the *comunidades eclesiales de base* [base Chrisitian communities — or
> CEBS] in the center of the city. . . . We had a group in the Guerrero colonia,
> a group of Christian women who were providing self-empowering train-
> ing sessions at the time. And there was interest in starting a project
> together with them and with EMAS. The earthquake, really, accelerated
> that project and our proposal. Our having seen how grave the situation
> was and what these colonias were going through, that EMAS gave them
> support — more of a day-to-day support in areas declared in emergency.

What was important to EMAS was being able to count on other organizations, not all necessarily women's organizations, but NGOs that pooled their
resources to help the victims of the earthquake.

We had the opportunity and the luck of having crossed paths with other people who valued our work and our support very much. They supported us in establishing a house, a center. They helped us purchase a house, a center, so that there we could tend to people more efficiently. And in that physical space, really, we founded what came to be called the Centro del Desarrollo Integral de la Mujer (Center for the Complete Development of Women or CEDIM), which came to be the crystallization of that joint project that I mentioned earlier between EMAS and the collective of women with whom we worked in the Guerrero colonia. . . . The physical space provided for meetings, larger gatherings, and workshops. . . . We worked a lot with them, and obviously with other women in what came to be the women's section of CUD, which was the Coordinadora Unica de Damnificados (the Unified Coordinating Group of [Earthquake] Trapped Victims). . . . That group was broadly based because many groups thought that it was necessary for us to coordinate ourselves in order to achieve, for example, the rehabilitation or construction of housing in as little time possible. There, as women of CUD, we organized a very important conference. With that conference, other women's organizations were formed representing the center of the city. There was, for example, the Unión Nueva de Tenochtitlán [New Union of Tenochtitlán], which was a mixed organization [consisting of both men and women].

Today the Unión Nueva de Tenochtitlán represents people primarily from the center of the city. Its women's section remains important for promoting political leadership. One of the founders of the Unión Nueva, Dolores Padilla Hernán, became a deputy in the Mexican Congress.

After 1985, the organizations that González Butrón described as forming in response to the earthquake were ones that trained leaders "so that they could participate in union organizations or in those related to the popular movement, urban or 'campesino' communities." Many "organized through workshops or meetings whether regional, national, or by sectors with objectives of consolidating leadership and promoting self-started organizations so that they could negotiate their demands with greater independence and within their groups" (Talamante Díaz, Careaga Pérez, and Parada Ampudia 1994: 8). The destruction of housing, the fear of another earthquake, and a preexisting ambivalence about the quality of life in Mexico City, with its growing crime and pollution, caused people like González Butrón to look to live elsewhere in Mexico. Consequently, in 1985, EMAS expanded its work beyond Mexico City, opening a branch in Morelia when González Butrón decided to move her family there.

RESHAPING THE WOMEN'S MOVEMENT IN MICHOACÁN

Prior to the early 1990s, few women's groups existed in Michoacán. Among the first to emerge was VenSeremos, a feminist collective that started with Fernanda Navarro, a philosophy professor at the Universidad Michoacana in 1982. Navarro began the feminist collective with students, four of whom were philosophy students from la Universidad Autónoma de México (UNAM), and friends and called it VenSeremos, a name that can be read several different ways, including "We Will Win" (*venceremos*), "Come, We Will Be" (*ven, seremos*), and "We Will Win/Be." In 1982, VenSeremos claimed thirty members and started a publication, *La Boletina* (The Bulletin), which gave birth to La Red Nacional de Mujeres (the National Women's Network). The idea for the bulletin and network was to create a space for a network of women to share feminist ideas. Of the twenty-one groups that joined La Red in 1982, today VenSeremos counts on eight (Ludec 2006:92). Until EMAS was founded in 1985, VenSeremos was the only organized women's group in Michoacán.

"My first organization in Morelia was VenSeremos in 1982," Navarro recalled. "We worked by linking ourselves with other groups outside of here [Morelia], because as it was then we knew of no other group [locally]. Later, when Maruja arrived, we established contacts with other [local] groups; we learned of EMAS and the networks that evolved [from then on]." Today, VenSeremos can count on many women's groups in addition to EMAS. In 1995, members of VenSeremos and philosophy faculty at the Universidad Michoacana established the university's Center for Gender Studies and Research (Centro de Estudios e Investigación de Género). And by 1995, when I started my research for this study, nineteen NGOs in Michoacán focused on women's issues.

In 1991 leaders of VenSeremos and the Center for Gender Studies and

Research formed the Taller Permanente de Estudios de la Mujer de la Escuela de Mujeres de la Universidad Michoacana, San Nicolás de Hidalgo (Permanent Research Group for Women's Studies at the Women's College of Michoacán University, San Nicolás de Hidalgo). Yadira Cira Gómez, one of the group's leaders, provided insight into its work.

I believe the group began after we started a research project in the School of Economics. That research focused on rural women's organizations, economic change, and women's status [in the home and in society]. The project touched on a number of areas, the economic, industrial, informal, and rural sectors. I . . . dedicated myself to rural women's situations. From this research we began to tease out theoretical questions concerning women, and we studied the question of gender a bit.

Since Cira Gómez already had worked with González Butrón in the university's School of Economics, the Taller brought issues raised by their research to EMAS. Thus, since the early 1980s, when VenSeremos held its first meetings, women had been organizing and using NGO spaces for mobilizing, consciousness-raising, and promoting research on women. In one decade, women's and feminist networks in Michoacán grew from one reflection group to a network of women's activist organizations with political influence in Michoacán and beyond.

Because of the link to EMAS, Cira Gómez and other students were able to learn about and join other women's NGO networks. She noted, in particular, the Red de ONGs de Mujeres del Estado de Michoacán (Women's NGO Network of the State of Michoacán), which advocated for democracy and political participation: "We analyze women's status and we try to follow the women's movement here in Michoacán and to participate actively in the movement, but in addition we seek to reach a level of understanding of the various perspectives of the larger feminist movement." Early on, therefore, the university women's group took on projects that members thought would help guide the feminist movement, but from the perspective of young women, a point of view that, Cira Gómez noted, was underrepresented in the feminist movement. The women who supported the Taller took up the challenge to add a feminist dimension to their work and contribute to larger feminist projects.

We decided that we had work to do in the School of Economics to bring out the point that there were other areas for research, particularly in areas affecting women, which often are not addressed in the traditional disciplines. Our approach is quite different than analyzing issues [and] making generalizations without looking specifically at how women suffer from their own particular situation as women, much of it stemming from economic problems. . . . So we took this line of [gender] inquiry and decided to work on that angle, by doing specific research projects to convince others that this was a wide-open area for research.

As a consequence of the Taller's work, the School of Economics broadened the discipline to include gender analyses.

According to Cira Gómez, the group studied how women are affected by labor market pressures, discrimination in the workplace, and sexual harassment. The Taller ultimately assumed a feminist perspective on women's issues, including challenging the traditional way students are trained to approach research in spaces such as the School of Economics. For Cira Gómez and other women of the Taller, the issue was not just what they would research but also how applying a gender lens would affect what they did with their findings. "During our research, a strong interest emerged in giving back to the women [they researched] a bit of what [we] found. We are finishing a video where we show images of the condition women live in. We try, first, not to abandon the work we did with rural women, by bringing back to them some of what they gave to us." Thus, for these women, activist feminist work identifies research on women with activism; it requires touching base with broad constituencies and understanding the political implications of doing so. For Cira Gómez and other women like her, gender consciousness first awakens in community work. The following narratives offered by leaders of women's NGOs show how the awakening happens and what leaders do to promote it in others.

The Political Approach   An interview with Concepción ("Coni") Torres of the Centro de Servicios Muncipales Heriberto Jara (Heriberto Jara Municipal Services Center, or CESEM) in Morelia underscored the importance of the links between women's activist networks in Michoacán and revealed the intricate way they evolved.

In 1979, 1980 I started by participating in the popular movement, beginning with my student days in student groups, organizing cultural festivals around the new Latin American [protest] music of the time. We organized activities with young people in the colonia where I lived on weekends and during the week with other groups of young people. Later, when I was a political science student at the Universidad Nacional Autónoma de México [National Autonomous University of Mexico, or UNAM], I became more deeply involved in the student movement out of which emerged an organization called the Unión de Ecologías Populares [Union of Popular Ecologies]. From that came several models for working in colonias, for creating political projects, and for political organizing. That is how I became involved in those organizations. Then, around 1988, 1989, I went to work in a women's organization, EMAS, when EMAS came here to Morelia.

As Torres reflected on her activism, she admitted that in her earlier years as an activist she had a class consciousness but not a gender one. Most of her work before she joined EMAS was in organizations that did not focus on women's issues. EMAS provided the first space for Torres and other women activists to discover the gender consciousness they were lacking, a consciousness Torres now says she puts at the center of all her activism, whether in EMAS or CESEM.

When Torres joined EMAS, started to read feminist writings, talk with González Butrón about women's issues, and link to other women's groups, particularly feminist ones, everything in her started to change. In Torres's words, she "began to acquire a gender consciousness."

It transforms your own relationship with your partner and with your children, because it became a very powerful total questioning [of everything I did]. Sometimes I feel that it all happened too fast. I questioned everything I did earlier, analyzing women's status in the whole country despite our numbers, and I saw myself reflected in many of the questions we were raising. It was not that the women's organizations present gender issues as though they were going to solve everything, but rather that I saw [gender issues] in the organizations I was a member of and I realized I was always in the shadows with my partner with regard to political participation. I saw in many of the participants women who were very brave but who were the "wives of so and so." In other words, you were not you for who you were, as your own person. Instead, you were the wife of a leader. We were their shadows, despite our own contributions, work, and building the movement.

Torres and other women often went home to partners who expected them to cook, iron, serve them, and take care of the children after coming home from meetings. Consequently, she said, they came to question the inequalities in their personal relationships and the disconnect with what they fought for in their political organizing. Participating in women's organizations changed these relationships and opened up new ways of thinking politically, particularly because many women began to raise gender issues in the political organizations where they worked with their men partners, as Torres did in CESEM. Many women like Torres remain active in mixed organizations like CESEM while also participating in women's NGOs like EMAS, but the women's organizations become the places where their gender consciousness awakens, and this consciousness is then brought to NGOs like CESEM.

These linkages have led women in Michoacán to propose a two-pronged approach to activism, continuing to work on broad community issues but linking these concerns to women's issues. Torres, for example, brought to CESEM her questioning of the absence of women's issues from rallies and influenced CESEM to call for an increased presence of women in government. Inspired by her achievements in transforming CESEM, Torres noted: "From that moment on, I say that I will never stop working in women's organizations, supporting their work whatever it is. . . . I went into my early years of activism with bandages over my eyes. Meeting and working with Maruja of EMAS was key to my political transformation. I value Maru a lot, I believe she has influenced me the most in my having acquired a gender consciousness."

These experiences echo those of other women activists. That is why network ties to women's organizations and to individual women activists who hold positions in multiple organizations are critical to understanding the empowerment of women in the Mexican women's movement. While Torres now spends most of her time in a mixed NGO, CESEM, her coming of age as a feminist has forever changed that group, as the maturation of others like her has changed other organizations. Today Torres, her husband, and other supporters of CESEM advocate for those frustrated with what was long Mexico's ruling party, the Partido Revolucionario Institucional (Institutional Revolutionary Party, or PRI) and lack of transparency in municipal and government elections. CESEM activists push for alternative forms of political representation. They hope to create a new political culture that will encourage Michoacán's, and Mexico's, citizens to reject corrupt politicians and in the process increase women's political participation and leadership. Whether CESEM realizes these goals or not, its objectives have been forever marked by the critical voices of women members who, in their own political awakenings, have come to consider gender issues central to the country's political discourse. The spectrum of these life trajectories in Michoacán goes beyond Torres.

Dulce Cortez of Mujeres por la Democracia (Women for Democracy) in Pátzcuaro, a small town outside Morelia, shares the political vision that Torres and CESEM have for Mexico. For over thirty years Cortez has worked with other women in Pátzcuaro to bring women's political voices into the public sphere. Around 1993, after working for years without a name for their group, they decided to call themselves Mujeres por la Democracia. Cortez and her colleagues began as members of the Partido de la Revolución Democrática (Party of the Democratic Revolution, or PRD). As Cortez recalls: "We belonged to one political party, the one we still belong to. For all the women it was important to support the party with their presence and to support the party's candidate. Women, at the community level, want change in government, and what they want is democracy. That is why they participate as members of this party." In relating the present activism of Mujeres por la Democracia to its past activities, Cortez noted the support the group received from other NGOs in the area, particularly those she saw as sharing its vision.

Many such links result from the presence of women's NGOs in these communities, particularly because of the community work they do in places like Pátzcuaro.

Information is exchanged that is of interest to the women [particularly information that highlights poor women's social condition throughout Mexico]. . . . These women see injustices and are frustrated that they are not heard, which they feel the Constitution of the Republic entitles them to be as a right. As we see it, all women have the right to good health, yet we live a lie and do not have the means to get help, especially in Pátzcuaro. [For example], in Pátzcuaro, there is a hospital for low-income people, but sometimes pregnant women have no one who will see them, or [doctors] charge them too much. That is why they "choose" to give birth in their homes, with the risks they run given their poor living conditions.

Thus the goals and objectives of Cortez and Mujeres por la Democracia entail advocating for democracy, a system that currently does not exist for poor women like Cortez. The social inequities they identify in their communities push them to activism in Mujeres por la Democracia. Most of the women members of this organization are peasant and indigenous women from Pátzcuaro who began by mobilizing out of specific community needs, urging local officials to address their demands. As the women began to meet around particular community issues, they began to see bigger opportunities to mobilize for social change by forming Mujeres por la Democracia. Their group is small and sometimes its only victory, according to Cortez, is that its members can come together, share information, and have others join them. But this in itself is worth all their effort. Thus, the members of Mujeres por la Democracia see networking and outreach, whether initiated by them or by other groups with which they collaborate, as opportunities to educate each other on issues that affect women. For Cortez, outreach is critical if women are to succeed in their goals.

The Outreach Approach Women who work for and support women's NGOs recognize the uphill battle they face in bringing their issues to center stage in Mexican politics. One problem they confront is reaching women and developing teaching strategies to raise gender consciousness and ultimately mobilize women into action. Some women activists have opted to work for women's rights via organizations directly focused on education, because they see education as the first step to developing gender consciousness. One woman committed to this strategy is Chela Sansón, who works for Mujeres del Magisterio Democrático (Women for Democratic Teaching). She is also a member of the Sindicato Nacional para Trabajadores de la Educación (the national teacher's union). But Sansón spends most of her time working with rural women, particularly those in the process of organizing themselves.

One group Sansón mentioned in particular was named after a woman leader of the Chiapas Zapatista movement:

Comandanta Ramona arose out of a need to organize women from different backgrounds, because of what they experience day-to-day and what the country is going through right now [economically and politically]. It is a support group. While it does not necessarily have a specific political definition, it is a group where women can identify as women . . . as political participants in society. My role in the group is to help organize, to participate, where people like me could do community work in efforts to help ourselves, but from within the community [beginning through education].

Sansón extends this political vision to her work with Mujeres del Magisterio Democrático, which is also linked to the work she does as a union activist, specifically in the area of education. For Sansón, the focus on education allows her to work on women's issues by training women to fight for goals like fair wages and work conditions. Sansón credits her union activism with giving her the opportunity in 1993 to work for Comandanta Ramona: "It was with the idea that we would organize ourselves as women, but beyond our roles in the home, to play a greater role in society, and linked to other women's organizations."

Another group, the Asociación Ayuda Mutua (Mutual Aid Association) realized that working with women on women's issues was critical to the organization, not only because of the number of women who participated in it but because women's issues were human rights issues. From its beginnings Ayuda Mutua focused on recovering the community's culture and art, as well as on educating children about the importance of caring for the environment. More recently Ayuda Mutua introduced human rights issues to its platform, concentrating on gender concerns and domestic and family violence. One of the group's leaders, Ana Santamaría Galván, noted:

It was obvious that we had to come to that, because the majority of the participants were women. Thus we have been giving that orientation, above all in working on human rights, where we've been the most successful. The other thing is that for the last three years we decided, along with several organizations, to put forth the first workshop on women in Michoacán. That project has been developing for three years, and only began in October of 1994. From that time up until now the main focus is on medical, psychological, and legal attention targeted to women. We also address two types of violence: family / domestic and sexual violence.

Ayuda Mutua's emphasis on domestic violence led to the creation of the Centro de Atención a la Mujer Violentada (Center for Battered Women, or CAMVI).

Among CAMVI's founders are members of other organizations in Michoacán's cluster of women's NGOs. Santamaría Galván noted, in particular, VenSeremos, EMAS, the Centro Michoacano de Investigación y Formación Vasco de Quiroga (Vasco de Quiroga Michoacán Center for Research and Training, or CEMIF, which shares its offices with EMAS), and the Pastoral Social (the local Catholic Church's social pastorate). CAMVI's supporters include leaders such as Maruja González Butrón and Ana Luisa Barajas of EMAS, Fernanda Navarro of VenSeremos, along women from the Pastoral Social. But particularly noteworthy here is the fact that CAMVI grew out of Ayuda Mutua's move to respond to domestic violence by promoting outreach and educating the public about the problem. For Santamaría Galván, organizations like CAMVI provide a space where NGOs focused on broader issues can narrow mobilization more effectively on issues like violence against women. She feels there is a need for this in societies that discourage public discussion of domestic violence.

The problem of [domestic] violence is a problem that has always existed in Michoacán, but there are times when it becomes more visible. It has to do with periods associated with political and economic crises. . . . In February 1991, which was when we began to crosslink the two organizations [Ayuda Mutua and CAMVI], we were working with rural and colonia women, and it was there we began to note the problem with [domestic] violence. . . . Denouncements of these acts began to appear in the local paper. And the question for us was what would be best to work specifically on that problem? It was then we began to develop a project that we later shared with other women [in the Michoacán women's NGO network]. Finally we concluded that it was necessary that this project not belong to just one organization, because of the magnitude of the work, but rather that it be done in collective support among a number of us, not just by providing services, but to sensitize people a bit [about the extent of the problem].

Santamaría Galván and others began with the goal of reducing and ultimately eliminating domestic violence. They first did research to learn the magnitude of the problem in Morelia and then moved to organizing. "We didn't have a lot of resources," said Santamaría Galván, "but we had a lot of energy and that was key — to have the commitment." Other groups began working on domestic violence in Michoacán, and it became important for Ayuda Mutua and CAMVI to network with them. "This permitted us to have more cohesion and uniformity in our strategies, as women, and in sharing ways we could approach the problem." To ensure that all the NGOs would continue working together, Santamaría Galván and others created a program around which to collaborate, not just giving each other emotional support but also pooling resources and offering legal assistance to women who came to seek help.

By July 1994, Santamaría Galván said, the collaborative efforts paid off: CAMVI, together with other local NGOs, opened an office to assist victims of domestic violence in Morelia.

At first, we felt that people were not coming. We were like vendors who had something to offer, but we had no takers. A center of this type was not reason for joy, because, well, violence is not natural. It should not exist, but on the other hand, there it was. . . . We knew how bad the problem was, but still the women did not come. In the first three to four months, we helped only about nineteen people. But after that the discussion group program began to grow and now every Wednesday at eleven in the morning we have a radio program that allows us to provide outreach to every state in the country. Discussions on violence are spreading, so much so that many have come to believe it is important, and our meetings are seeing more people. A lot of women are coming, including some men and children, which tells us the degree to which we have a problem.

In addition to the radio program, the women write a newspaper column, which appears on Sundays in the local paper, on domestic and family violence. As demand for CAMVI's services increased, so too did the community work.

Because Santamaría Galván and her colleagues feared they were not reaching enough people, they decided to support a number of other community projects, particularly around workshops, and increased the number of venues where they could do this. Consequently, they have been invited to schools. For Santamaría Galván, this is a measure of their success: "We are reaching people more, at the community level, and in reaching them, we are having them learn more about these issues — we think from there we will be able to do a bit more."

The Ecological Approach Women's NGO outreach programs also extend to the environment, in particular to how environmental issues touch women's lives. Asociación Ecologista Viva Natura (Viva Natura Ecologist Association) arose out of demands for more attention to larger environmental issues. According to Elena Alvarez Ugena,

> twelve years ago a strong tradition to save our natural resources emerged in Michoacán. . . . Education about the environment was the principal focus — raising consciousness, analyzing the city's sprawling growth [referring to Uruapán, a city about two hours from Morelia] and how it posed environmental problems, which eventually required suspending several city projects. . . . The focus [in the beginning] was on urban growth or any initiative that affected the environment, offering alternatives to proposals that we deemed harmful to the environment.

Those who founded Viva Natura had already been working in different ways on saving the environment. They realized early on that being an NGO would give them a formal status allowing them to organize around environmental issues more efficiently, as a recognized political entity. In addition, being an NGO allowed them to raise money by applying for grants as an organization and to disseminate information as part of an education strategy.

According to Alvarez Ugena, from the beginning they worked with few resources, almost always using their own money and that of their members. For a while it worked. "It gave us a lot of independence; we didn't have any commitments to entities outside [the organization]." As I argue in chapter 4, outside funding often influences the focus and energies of NGOs because it entails a commitment to work on issues important to the funders. Like many NGOs, Viva Natura has faced financial problems, particularly during national economic crises like that of the mid-1990s. In these moments the NGO's members, hard pressed to make ends meet at home, find it even more difficult to find money to give the organization. Consequently, Viva Natura turned to outside funding, particularly for its project of educating people about the environment—a significant part of the group's work. Alvarez Ugena provided the following overview of the organization's efforts.

We started by working within Michoacán [at the state level] in the Forum de Medio Ambiente y Desarrollo [Forum for the Environment and Development]. Sustainable development was one of the central points of the forum. Lately we have become involved in development and a proposal for the environment section [of the forum], producing a human rights letter that would be taken to the next national meeting [on the environment], where they are going to be reading a number of letters on human rights where for the first time the environment is included.

The 1995 forum was important because it was part of a series of organizing efforts to bring national attention to the environment. The first Forum de Medio Ambiente y Desarrollo had taken place seven years earlier. Though it took place in Michoacán, the 1988 meeting was in reality a national meeting organized by Viva Natura. "It was the first broadly based NGO meeting on the environment," Alvarez Ugena said. "For many, the 1988 meeting was a success: we charged nothing to participants for attending, and because the conference was free, we were able to get a large number of participants."

About four hundred people attended the three-day conference. From these first mobilizing efforts, Viva Natura has grown, linking women's issues to environmental issues on a broader scale.

Alvarez Ugena saw Viva Natura's school and its efforts to raise consciousness as essential to the group's promotion of a healthy environment: "I believe that one of the cornerstones of the problem is rooted in the system of patriarchy." In fact, Alvarez Ugena's coming to environmental activism via feminist activism exemplifies the link ecofeminists see between the status of women in a society and that society's attitude toward the environment. "Like multicultural and global feminism, ecofeminism strives to show the connections among all forms of human oppression, and because women have been culturally tied to nature, ecofeminists argue there are conceptual, symbolic, and linguistic connections between feminist and ecological issues" (Tong 1998: 246). Alvarez Ugena has become an environmental activist without abandoning the women's movement, because as she noted they are connected.

> I had already come from doing feminist work in Morelia . . . with a small group at first when I was teaching at the university there. It had no name [referring to the first feminist organization she participated in, twenty years earlier] in fact it was more like a study group. Unfortunately, I voluntarily left the university because I had other interests, and I didn't continue formally in a feminist organization. . . . I believe that since I was small I have been a rebel against the system. I lived the problems of having been born a woman. . . . I studied in a typically male career to put it bluntly, chemical engineering. It was a challenge at that time. We were five women in that part of the school at the university. I lived through a lot of problems, and I believe that in many respects this shaped who I am with a consciousness about discrimination toward women. That segregation [being a woman in a man's world] followed me in my work with environmentalist organizations, and not just the segregation, but the limitations that a *machista* and patriarchal vision imposes on both men and women.

Alvarez Ugena noted that environmental movements often miss the link between gender and environmental issues. Consequently, when the Mac-

Arthur Foundation called for projects on women and the environment, Alvarez Ugena found the possibility of such a grant to be very attractive: "I was waiting for an opportunity to work linking those two issues [the environment and gender], and so I took one of my old ideas for developing a project, and it was funded."

The MacArthur Foundation grant allowed her to focus on the general theme of women and the environment. The project was to create a school to empower women as advocates for their own development, the environment, and the community. This, Alvarez Ugena noted, is why "the education program of the school is very clear that our idea is to link perspectives of gender to the environment." The school came to be called Escuela de Desarrollo de la Mujer, el Ambiente y la Comunidad (School for Development of Women, the Environment, and the Community). The story of Viva Natura's emergence underscores another dimension of feminist networks in NGOs: that leaders often come to one movement via experiences in other movements. This is a pattern I noted earlier in interviews with Coni Torres of CESEM and Maruja González Butrón of EMAS. The EMAS history is particularly noteworthy given González Butrón's position not just in Morelia's NGO community, but nationally and internationally. Her role in preparations for the Fourth World Conference on Women in Beijing in 1995, as well as her position in women's faith-based communities, shows the overlap of NGOs with religious groups.

The Religious Approach   EMAS's history in Morelia began with the efforts of González Butrón, supported by a small group of women who shared her vision. EMAS also is linked to CEMIF, founded by González Butrón's husband, the late liberation theologian Raúl Vidales. The mission of CEMIF has been to advocate for the popular sector of Michoacán. EMAS has promoted an activism nurtured by the Catholic social teaching so important to González Butrón, particularly the liberation theology her husband espoused in his life and writings. To understand the underlying feminist Christian principle advocated by EMAS since its origin, I asked González Butrón to tell me how she came to the women's movement and connected it to a type of liberation theology. The history she provided underscores the complex ways in which organizations emerge and how the trajectories of individuals who come to these NGOs bring potential for links across movements no matter how unlikely given, for example, feminist critiques of the patriarchy embedded in most religious traditions.

González Butrón began as a student activist in Catholic organizations, which led her to broader social activism and ultimately to the women's movement. Her path to the latter passed through participation in Mujeres para el Diálogo—the feminist Christian organization that I mentioned briefly in the introduction and will discuss further in chapter 3.

I began to participate in [the women's] movement a long time ago, but specifically with women around 1981. Before that I had participated in mixed Christian groups, the Juventud Estudiantil Católica, the Unión de Estudiantes Católicos [Catholic Student Youth and Union of Catholic Students, two organizations rooted in Catholic Action, a progressive movement that took root in Latin America in the 1940s and 1950s and that more recently was associated with liberation theology]. After that, [I participated] in what here [in Mexico] in 1981 was known as the Acción Solidaria de los Cristianos [Christians' Action in Solidarity], where I began to participate in a women's collective specifically focused on women's issues. It seemed to me very important to participate, because after all I began to observe with a number of women, the sheer number of them, who were active in several social movements. They were a majority and yet, as in political parties and other organizations, there were no women leaders. I felt the same occurred in the Christian movements, those embedded in the church movements; it was then that I came to understand the connection. At the invitation of Mujeres para el Diálogo I entered into a second phase [of my life]. Mujeres para el Diálogo was founded during the bishops' conference in Puebla [1979], and it was at that time I decided to get involved [in the women's movement]. With that experience of coming to understand a bit the specific problems women have to confront, a militancy toward the women's movement surged in me.

González Butrón also discussed the uphill battle women faced in beginning their push for their rights within church institutions.

We tried through various efforts to reflect, as a movement of Christian women, with deliberate intent to develop strategies to bring about change within our churches. It is in this sphere where today I find myself very alone and why I appreciate being in other venues, like those offered by other women like Alma Tamez, a member of the Asociación de Pastoras [Association of Women Pastors, an organization composed mainly of Protestant women] in Mexico City, . . . Together with other women, we try to open spaces for Christian women, many of them Catholic from Guanajuato, Aguascalientes, to express and share the same uneasiness that I do, . . . but I realize how differently we see the world and our situation within our own church. . . . There are so few of us working in this area, and we face so many challenges that we haven't been able to push ahead.

Despite those frustrations, González Butrón and others in EMAS have found support for their work with a local Catholic women's group, from Michoacán's diocesan pastoral service. Beginning in the mid-1980s, EMAS established a careful relationship with women of the Centro de Apoyo a la Salud Alternativa (Center for Support of Alternative Health, or CASA) from the pastoral social programs of Morelia's Catholic Church. The relationship is precarious because the women are always conscious that the Catholic Church oversees and can reject any of their community projects. But for EMAS opening avenues for dialogue and collaboration among women's organizations is crucial to community outreach and diversity, which can strengthen women's feminist networks.

To learn more about CASA's work I conducted a collective interview with the leadership of CASA in June 1995. I asked about the community work they did. They identified a number of areas of emphasis. These included health, creating cooperatives (particularly for marketing goods produced by women), food programs, and farming. A number of the women of CASA study alternative medical practices and nutrition so they can teach poor women how to prepare healthy meals at low cost. They also teach women how to make clothing so poor families can become self-sufficient. The object for CASA is for its teaching methods and the process of learning to empower women so they in turn will teach others. For students, the experience should create a sense of community that can be the basis for learning how to help themselves and how to mobilize their communities.

Ironically, the women of CASA began through the initiative of a local priest, Father Roberto. Beatriz Guerrero, who was concerned with the poor nutrition of the local population, gave Father Roberto materials on the use of soy-based products to teach women how to make cheap, nutritious meals. In our interview, one of the CASA leaders noted: "That was the beginning [of CASA], later they taught other small groups, first in the parish and then outside the parish. After a while, he [Father Roberto] decided to leave the parish to dedicate himself exclusively to working in the area of health and nutrition; after that we expanded to include teaching women how to make clothing." In addition to Father Roberto, CASA's founders included Beatriz Guerrero, Carmen Ortega, Olga Trejo, Benita Ramos, Elba Morales, Leonor León, and Refugio García. Since those first days and the initial emphasis on teaching about nutrition and health, the women of CASA have supported several new projects. Today CASA in turn enjoys the support of several women's groups, including a number from Mexico City. These other women's NGOs help by providing sewing machines and other materials that CASA needs for its grassroots work. CASA's success in the communities surrounding Morelia has enabled it to join other groups in hosting local, regional, and national meetings. This strategy of exchanging and disseminating information maintains high levels of interaction and sharing of resources among NGOs, both in Morelia and in greater El Paso/Ciudad Juárez, as I will discuss further in the next chapter.

One aspect of CASA that is particularly important to our discussion is its faith-based activism. "Our work comes out of faith, our Christian commitment, and out of the reality we live" (CASA group interview). This aspect of CASA's background is a little-discussed element of women's activism and is thus important to document. The women of CASA began to organize in parish social service activities and from there generated community-based, self-sustained, self-directed projects. From teaching nutrition and health, they learned and taught organic agricultural methods and in the process increased their own awareness and others' of how they had come to depend on commercial pesticides. Several of the CASA leaders noted the pressure small farmers are put under to grow what is lucrative instead of what their families need to eat. Consequently, many farmers borrow from banks to pay for pesticides and, when crops fail, find themselves unable to feed their families and in debt. The women of CASA seek to increase people's capacity to feed themselves: "it is about being rooted in people's social reality, that they be able to live in dignity, and be subjects of their own destiny," whether they live in the semiurban, rural, or indigenous communities of Michoacán.

Also, we cannot ignore women's commitment to church work with the popular sectors of Michoacán, or the call some women feel for a "preferential option" to work with the poor. This was term used at the 1979 Conferencia Episcopal Latinoamericana (Latin American Bishops' Conference, or CELAM) in Puebla. Church community leaders use it as a banner for the type of community work that the women of CASA and EMAS are engaged in, which for them raises consciousness on commitment to the poor and, for many, the particular way poverty touches women's lives compared to men's. I will discuss this more extensively in chapter 3, which focuses on faith-based community activism. Faith-based activism in this context helps us to understand why the coordinators of CASA would take what they learn in health and nutrition to their parish work. For them the church is "a living church, a poor people's church, where we work toward a lived faith" committed to social activism (CASA group interview). As one of the women of CASA put it, faith-based activism is about making commitments and doing the type of community work where we "become active agents of change."

Some of the CASA leaders remembered when they first felt called to be agents of change. For one woman this moment came during an international women's forum: "To go forth and transform women who have in their hands the knowledge and skills that both men and women have and have had for centuries, and that we are recognizing only today, goes beyond their homes to the communities where women participate. It is very important work, to promote women . . . with more dignity. This has created problems in the minds of some . . . because of the machismo that we have."

Because they confront machista attitudes, CASA women recognize the importance of the women's movement for transforming their communities and the Catholic Church. Men feel threatened by the women's activism. According to one woman of CASA: "The men say, 'Well, go for it: you want liberation, take the reins.' They do not get it, because they say, 'You want to be equals, then you can work like men.'" So while the women see changes, they also see that people's views are still tempered by traditional attitudes.

Another CASA leader also noted that while women have increasing opportunities to play leadership roles in the Catholic Church, they must still get permission from the local priest for many of their community projects. For many of these women, the problem lies in the patriarchal attitudes embedded in the minds of many priests. As one of the women from CASA commented: "We live in one of the most conservative states of the Republic. It is a small number of priests who are with us; the majority of them are very conservative." Despite these obstacles, women continue to do their community work, finding support in other women's organizations, particularly EMAS and women leaders like González Butrón, who share with them a faith-based approach. Suffice it to say here that for the women of CASA having EMAS and González Butrón in Michoacán has made a difference. For many of these NGOs women's networks provide not only opportunities to exchange information and resources but also support for community work in what for many are hostile environments, particularly when the work focuses on women. To lessen antagonism toward their work locally, many of the women's NGOs try to raise gender consciousness while tackling what are crisis issues for their communities. Consequently, health is a focus for groups like CASA and the Equipo de Promoción a la Salud Comunitaria (Community Health Promotion Team, or EPROSCO).

The Health Approach EPROSCO began its work in 1988, though it was legally instituted as a civil association (the legal status for NGOs in Mexico) in 1990. Delia Villalobos, one of the group's founding members, told its early history:

> We began to work first with small groups in a community [in Michoacán], then that same community began to see the benefits of working around health and that opened other opportunities in other communities, including in other regions [outside Michoacán], and so we grew. We thought that it would be more beneficial to constitute ourselves as a civil association to have some structure and to have legal recognition for our work. At first, we were about eight women and a priest who was a

sociologist. . . . We decided we wanted to work in the area of health. Some of us were working in the Pastoral Social but then decided that we no longer wanted to work under the church's domain.

The fact that Villalobos left the church social programs to start a separate organization is not unusual. NGOs are often spin-offs of the efforts of other groups, in this case a community health project.

From then on, we supported health projects on the prevention of illnesses, at first on the social aspects of it, then the biological, then clinical, therapeutic. . . . These were the key areas. Then almost from the beginning we began promoting the idea of forming health groups where women could reflect on health issues, their own as well as the community's. But, overall, we could say that our projects have been on promoting health in general, community pharmacies, medicinal herb gardens, in other words, all that is related to health, which for us has many aspects.

From the start, Villalobos added, women were interested in self-help, in learning how to make their own medicines and about alternative, more affordable medicines: "It was like that was all the women cared about." Much of EPROSCO's work focused on teaching alternative medicine and how to care for oneself.

Today, in addition to alternative medicine, EPROSCO teaches communities ways to fight malnutrition and stay healthy. It also has moved from working exclusively on health issues to opening discussion of women's marginalization in society and the relationship of this marginalization to specific health problems also rooted in other social problems that affect especially poor women. As Villalobos put it, health "is about more than learning how to make remedies; it is also something to be analyzed—what are its root causes." Analyzing the structural causes of illness leads us to question how and why Mexican society is structured in such a way that poor people are bartered in a global economic system where the rich benefit and the poor are exploited and made sick. For Villalobos, this questioning has helped women, particularly peasant and indigenous women, who are rarely given the chance to reflect on and ask questions about their social condition. "No one really gives them opportunities to look at their lives," Villalobos said, "to talk about them, and to ask questions that lead women to recognize how limited their lives have been in terms of their opportunities, for having space to talk about the different type of abuse they experience in their lifetimes." For women like Villalobos, EPROSCO is an empowering space for women who never thought they could receive an education or become health teachers in their communities. In doing so, they are put in situations where they begin not only to develop class consciousness but also to raise questions that often lead to gender consciousness. NGOs like EPROSCO allow women to question their status in their families and society, first by asking why women receive less formal education than men. The questioning evolves as they learn to read and as they train to become community health workers. Women working in NGOs like EPROSCO begin to ask themselves why educational opportunities came so late in their lives. From their experiences in the NGOs, women learn to reach out to others, often first by disseminating information about their own organization's work.

Consequently, NGOs use their networks to exchange ideas, strategize, expand resources, and reach out farther into the state of Michoacán. Villalobos mentioned EMAS (both in Michoacán and in Mexico City) as an NGO with which EPROSCO maintains strong ties. She also noted relationships with the "national health movement, so we have relationships with people in other states, including Oaxaca, Tabasco, Veracruz, Sonora, Nuevo León, and Jalisco. We cover about eight regions [including Mexico City]." The extent of this networking underscores not only the level of exchange and communication among the NGOs but also the degree to which health issues became a basis for mobilization in Michoacán. Mobilizing around AIDS has created opportunities not only to raise consciousness about a major health problem for the people of Michoacán, given the large percentage of the state's population that migrates to and from the United States, a journey during which many contract HIV/AIDS, but also about AIDS as a gender issue.

Michoacanos Unidos por la Salud y Contra el Sida, A.C. (Michoacanos United for Health and against AIDS Inc., or MUSSAC), based in Morelia, leads the effort to raise awareness of AIDS as a gender issue. The leader and cofounder Yolanda Pineda noted that from the beginning "MUSSAC included a focus on women's health, because health issues are central to women's concerns," particularly because as men migrate to the United States, some contract AIDS and, when they return home, expose their partners to the disease, often not knowing that they themselves have it. But MUSSAC is not strictly a women's NGO: AIDS has hit Michoacán's gay community (and its prostitutes) the hardest. Consequently, beginning in 1990 but more forcefully after 1993, when the organization received its official not-for-profit NGO status, MUSSAC began working out of Morelia to inform the public about AIDS. "I was the one who provided the first opportunity to do work on AIDS here in Michoacán in 1987," Pineda noted, "when I was part of the Secretariat of Health. This problem of AIDS touches three essential levels: life, sexuality, and death. It is in a constant cycle. Sometimes it is not easy, because we confront ourselves, our sexuality, and our prejudices." At first MUSSAC focused on working with a number of groups from the gay community and with prostitutes, because "they were the most vulnerable."

As time passed, Pineda said, MUSSAC found it necessary to include other groups. "We started to invite people committed to people [affected by AIDS], who we thought could give their time; so we invited doctors, social workers, nurses, housewives, and we started this organization with twenty people." MUSSAC's work expanded beyond the gay and prostitute community, because members of the organization realized the extent of the AIDS epidemic among heterosexuals, particularly women exposed to AIDS by male migrant partners.

In the beginning we supported projects to continue working with the gay community and with prostitute groups. . . . They are the vulnerable and stigmatized groups, and we accomplished a lot there. Afterward, we realized that we had more to learn. . . . We realized that there was a large heterosexual population, above all young housewives infected by migrants to the United States. . . . These were vulnerable groups. So we started working with them, developing strategies to work with them. Now we are preoccupied with working directly with these women. We have to approach this carefully, because we live in a very machista society where women have all the disadvantages in the world.

Pineda refers here to the difficulty of working with women in a way that does not threaten their relationships with their families and larger communities, given the tendency in patriarchal systems to blame women when they contract diseases associated with sexual promiscuity. For Pineda and others in MUSSAC the challenge is to develop strategies to disseminate to an often unsuspecting and misinformed population information about how one can avoid contracting AIDS. The stereotype is that AIDS is limited to people engaged in "immoral behavior."

MUSSAC teaches against these stereotypes and prejudices, showing that the victims of AIDS include women and the children to whom they give birth. They also include the widows of men who die from AIDS, women who are rejected by their community when it becomes public that they are either infected with or part of a family exposed to AIDS. Pineda and others at MUSSAC take on AIDS as a human rights problem. To fight ignorance, MUSSAC supporters disseminate information and direct much of their efforts at the most isolated rural communities, informing them about AIDS by using pamphlets with vignettes. This strategy allows MUSSAC to target women, because as Pineda noted the organization wants not only to inform people and do outreach in the most marginalized communities, "we want women to become aware of all the projects that they can become active in," to mobilize them around a health problem where they are likely to become a victim.

MUSSAC also targets university students, particularly women. The strategy here is to recruit from an educated young population, one also at risk for AIDS. MUSSAC also sees these young educated women as possible recruits for AIDS education, since they tend to work on other social issues. But most of MUSSAC's support comes from networking with other NGOs. In fact, the leadership of MUSSAC sees networking with other NGOs as part of its mission. Networking strength around health issues was reflected in interviews with heads of other NGOs in Michoacán. For example, EMAS and González Butrón in particular were mentioned as key to the overlapping relationships that these health-focused NGOs depend on for their grassroots mobilization. The networking is such that individuals who work in various NGOs in the network often move among the organizations. For example, Cira Gómez, who I mentioned earlier as a leader of the Taller Permanente de Estudios de la Mujer at the Universidad Michoacana's Escuela de Mujeres and a member of EMAS, moved to work full-time in the Centro de Estudios

Sociales y Ecológicos (Center for Social and Ecological Studies, or CESE) in Pátzcuaro, Michoacán.

CESE is a mixed (men's and women's) NGO, one of whose objectives is working on women's issues. CESE started as an environmental NGO primarily mobilized around the contamination of the local lake (Lake Pátzcuaro) and its tributaries. Because one of the town's primary industries is fishing, its livelihood depends on the health of the lake. Consequently, CESE's main support comes from local fishermen. According to Consuelo Suárez, one of the women organizers of CESE, CESE's work first started with the fishermen, and it continue to work with them, but later it

moved to work with artisans. . . . After some time there came a moment in CESE where the funders began to ask, 'Where are the women?' At that time, there were two women working here and so they [CESE] decided to do a project on women, taking inventory of the region, and from that they learned about women's needs. The focus of study noted health issues. . . .

Suárez added:

Consequently, it was in 1987 that I came in to develop a project [with a focus on women]. We put together a project, sent it [to funding agencies], and it turned out that within six months they approved it. . . . From there we located women organizers . . . from the communities of La Rivera. We started working with them and then we saw that the work in this area [women and health] kept growing, becoming more accepted, but we didn't have adequate personnel to manage and give it full attention, and so in CESE we decided to train two of our women members from the communities so that they could give it full attention. That is how we started and later, instead of just two organizers, we saw the group expand into new areas of work and in several different communities. We eventually grew to have three [full-time] women community organizers.

By 1995, the women's section of CESE was fully committed to promoting health as a primary area of focus. According to Suárez, it was the area that had taken CESE the most time to develop. "It has consumed the women [of

CESE] and me as well; we've done a systemization and theorizing of the experience, which we felt we needed and are working with Cira Gómez of EMAS in doing that." For Suárez the self-reflection was important because much of the work with women is with indigenous and peasant women. Pátzcuaro is, after all, in the heart of indigenous Purépecha rural communities. The proximity to those communities shapes the work of CESE and other local NGOs focused on these communities' concerns. The overlapping interests among these local NGOs lead them to share resources and move personnel across organizations. Cira Gómez knew of and worked with CESE long before she became a full-time staff member. Like many NGOs in the region, CESE and EMAS often cosponsor events that engage a number of women's communities, including those of indigenous and peasant women.

The Indigenous Approach EMAS's relationship with CESE, their exchange of information and resources, including personnel, shows how indigenous women's groups came to shape the women's movement in Michoacán. As I have discussed, such relationships often grow out of historical events that impact the national women's movement and out of the geographic movement of NGOs and their personnel around the country. In the case of EMAS, the opportunities for alliances with indigenous women's groups came with its move to Michoacán after the 1985 earthquake in Mexico City. Shortly after arriving in Morelia, González Butrón met Tomasa Sandoval, a founder of Mujeres Grupo Erandi de Pichátaro (Erandi Women's Group of Pichátaro) and a prominent figure in the Nación Purépecha (Purépecha Nation), an indigenous organization that fights for the rights of indigenous people throughout Mexico. Sandoval established strong ties with EMAS, introducing EMAS to the Purépecha women of her community and legitimating EMAS in the eyes of the Purépecha.

Thanks to the Mujeres Grupo Erandi, Purépecha women showed EMAS members the importance of linking gender issues with those of ethnicity, a connection the Mexican women's movement did not begin to understand until the early 1980s. As I discussed in the introduction, this shift began in 1980 with the first Encuentro Nacional de Mujeres (National Women's Gathering) in Mexico City, which changed the national women's movement from one mostly limited to university-based feminists to one that drew its strength from the grassroots. González Butrón underscored this understanding of the power of diversity: "Perhaps something that I have taken great care of in these last few years is that in the spaces where I work with women and in those that are mixed we never leave aside the gender perspective. . . . we must also . . . take into account all the characteristics of ethnicity. We believe, for example, that the birth of indigenous organizations and our incorporation into these other different spaces are very important." The presence and political articulations of Michoacán's Purépecha community have made their mark on Mexican NGOs.

The effort to win political recognition of indigenous people in Michoacán and throughout Mexico has a long history. The struggle for land and against political and economic marginalization is a common theme in Mexico's peasant history (Velázquez 1992). But the history of Mexico's indigenous people and that of its broader peasantry are not identical: since the colonial period, class and gender domination have marginalized indigenous people in particular ways. Change only became possible for indigenous women in the early and mid-1970s, when a series of government actions, especially the creation of bilingual schools, encouraged indigenous people to preserve their cultures and languages. According to Margarita Velázquez (1992), a new indigenous leadership emerged during this period. The indigenous movement nationwide and in Michoacán specifically was strengthened by indigenous professionals and university students. Many of these professionals affirmed their commitment to the indigenous cause and became leaders in the movement. Sandoval and her husband, also a Purépecha, are two examples. Tomasa Sandoval began to question and to challenge the social conditions that indigenous women faced both outside and inside their communities. She mobilized a number of women in her community to organize other Purépecha women to address some of their problems. According to Sandoval, this is how Mujeres Grupo Erandi began, as an effort to empower indigenous women:

Basically, we started our work around workshops, courses, course-workshops on women and health, on illnesses that more commonly strike women. [Also], on how to educate children, the rights of children, women's rights, psychological well-being, and women's sexuality, which more or less was done through the Grupo Erandi. More or less we took those approaches. In other areas, we focused on practical things, developing vegetable gardens, raising pigs, chickens. . . . That is what we did, the courses, talks, particularly courses on empowering women, and also workshops on alternative nutrition focused on the use of soy products, taking from the bean its milk and meat substitutes. . . . Our goal was to try and have this alternative nutrient made integral to their diets, for the children, and most of all made affordable for the men and women of Pichátaro, who are peasant farmers. Women for the most part are not salaried workers. They dedicate themselves to working in the home, doing housework, and making artisanal products to sell in local markets. So our projects are meant to give women information on how they can, with few resources, feed their children.

Mujeres Grupo Erandi became an opportunity for indigenous women to discuss their experiences as women.

Sandoval was proud that the exchanges have led to the group's recording of its activities and the community projects it has supported. She noted that the group had no resources, and yet the women took from their own weekly budgets what they needed to support Grupo Erandi projects, including bus trips to town meetings. Sandoval felt this was important in the process of empowering these indigenous women, many of whom were never taught to read, as most in their families assumed that their sole purpose was to marry and have children. In their patriarchal societies, the goal was to invest in the education of boys, who would grow up to be the heads of household and community leaders. "You see the effects of this attitude," Sandoval said, "when, of those [women] who attend meetings, at best four know how to read." When a document has to be signed to support a project or event, one of the women leaders signs the document on behalf of all of them. Sandoval found this painful:

To realize that women always follow men at a disadvantage and that as long as we do not raise consciousness of the fact that we have to unite, organize, and battle for equal rights together, we are limited. [To organize, we need] not necessarily . . . university degrees, but at least . . . elementary, high school, or technical ones, so we can challenge the problems we face economically and politically in Mexico. We need to be prepared to push for a more humane life, as mothers, partners, and children.

She was heartened by the activism made possible by collaborating with groups like EMAS: "We would like to make miracles, to have a lot of arms like an octopus."

One example, Sandoval said, was Grupo Erandi's literacy classes for women and EMAS's role in helping to make them happen: "EMAS is important in providing assistance with training and providing . . . tools to teach people to read." Even small efforts such as these, she noted, have other effects, particularly in the lives of women who have so much working against them: "The women, even though they might not know how to read, have gained a new concept of life, their personhood, and society at large, that for us is occasion to celebrate, to have, even for a little while, some satisfaction of knowing that we have contributed to producing even some change in the women" by teaching them to read and subsequently to reflect on the conditions that limit them. The change is visible, Sandoval said, when one visits the women in their homes or workplaces and compares their attitudes to those of women who are not participating in NGOs like Mujeres Grupo Erandi:

> About two months ago some women researchers from Mexico City, one of them doing her doctorate and the other her masters, visited us in the community and conducted interviews comparing women who were active in NGOs and those who were not. . . . the researchers found . . . that the concept toward life of those in groups like Erandi is different from those who are not in any organized group. This is what gives me pleasure . . . , to know that we have projects that are making a difference.

Despite this sense of victory, Sandoval also noted the obstacles the government creates to obtaining funding for some of her group's projects. She observed that if CEMIF and EMAS had not provided resources, Mujeres Grupo Erandi would not be able to do some of its community work. This is one example of how essential collaboration among NGOs is to getting what little funding and support they receive.

In other words, NGO networking helps to sustain community work. Even when funding is limited or nonexistent, NGOs can bring broad-based pressure on local, state, and federal agencies to support community projects. "Some of our supporters have gone with us to Morelia," Sandoval said, "to the city hall, to help gain support [for our causes]." Through collaboration, Mujeres Grupo Erandi has obtained donations and bank credits to build a place for the women to mill grain so they can make and sell tortillas. Other efforts have led to the opening of cooperative community grocery stores. The goal for a number of the NGOs is to make food available and to provide low-interest loans so people can buy food. In other instances, the groups seek funding to purchase basic materials needed to make marketable products locally — including embroidered tablecloths, blouses, and dresses — to build up communal funds.

Because indigenous communities are known for their embroidery, organizations like Mujeres Grupo Erandi have sought to sell these products through cooperatives, allowing them to market their goods effectively and at the same time protect women's wages by selling their products only as part of a cooperative. Although "we have not made a lot of money up till now," Sandoval said, "we've been recovering our initial investments, and our utopian ideal is to forge ahead as women, not so much to make money. . . . in supporting these projects we have come to realize something bigger." Thus, for Sandoval and the women of Mujeres Grupo Erandi, the primary goal is to help indigenous women value themselves as women and as full citizens of a society that has marginalized them. Consequently, Mujeres Grupo Erandi sees empowerment workshops as ways "to fortify an organization of diverse women, not just Purépechas, but other indigenous women, and ultimately all women."

For Mujeres Grupo Erandi, Sandoval said, the motivation to collaborate with nonindigenous women's groups arose out of slowly broadening awareness, from one of their condition as indigenous people to one of their condition also as women:

In indigenous communities, above all among the more remote ones, you see the worst economic conditions. It is where we have the highest indicators of malnutrition among children. So, with the mothers of these children, we try to organize workshops on health, better nutrition by focusing on alternative foods, and other projects like that. Basically, our goal has been to promote organizations, to foster organizations that promote community self-help programs, particularly from a gender perspective. This is what most attracts the women, because it is the most unfamiliar to us. For us indigenous women, it [gender consciousness] is what we least take into account, and often do not value, even among ourselves, because we do not even know we have that right.

Linking indigenous women's situation to other women's experiences, Sandoval believes that women will need to mobilize in joint efforts if gender and feminist consciousness is really to make a difference for the women's movement. It is important to remember that although Sandoval and other Purépecha women are embedded in the indigenous movements of Mexico, working with local women's NGOs has led them to organize their own indigenous women's groups. "So long as we do not . . . organize and unite with more women," Sandoval said, "this challenge or that utopian ideal will not be possible. In a recent women's NGO gathering, they called three of us from Grupo Erandi to come to the meeting, and we went because we consider that with more women, and not just indigenous women, we will move ahead politically and overcome the great obstacles that many of us women face."

Sandoval and NGOs like Mujeres Grupo Erandi underscore what the World Conference on Women in Beijing would show the world. The preparations for the conference helped to bring out an already evolving relationship between Purépecha and non-Purépecha women; among women's NGOs and mixed ones; among local, regional, and state NGOs; and among these groups and international organizations. As the women's NGO networks of Michoacán show, there is potential strength in women's movements guided by an emerging multicultural and global feminism. This would become clearer throughout 1994 and 1995 as women's NGOs in Michoacán and elsewhere prepared for Beijing.

When the "Toward Beijing" efforts began in Michoacán, the Purépecha people, peasant groups, and women already had made gains through community projects. At least two indigenous women's NGOs — Mujeres Grupo Erandi de Pichátaro and Grupo de Mujeres Juchari Ambe de Cherán (Juchari Ambe Women's Group of Cherán) — were already active and easy to recruit to the Beijing preparations, since local women's NGO networks were already established and had achieved some level of exchange.

The women's NGOs in Michoacán created the State Coordinating Committee of Women's NGOs in order to strengthen and expand their networks with goals that would take them beyond Beijing. The State Coordinating Committee's documents show that women's NGOs used the opportunity to help them mobilize at a state level, making them more efficient at advancing their interests locally. The NGOs moved to create a large, broad-based, and politically prominent women's movement in Michoacán. The documents highlight these groups' commitment to work on gender issues while at the same time advancing the interests of popular and indigenous sectors of their communities by emphasizing class and race issues. The Michoacán women's movement was a microcosm of the national women's movement in that it linked groups working in different areas. It was embedded in several national political fronts: indigenous, peasant, labor, and environmental issues, as well as confrontations with a national political party (the PRI) that had restricted the political opportunities of these constituencies. As I have shown in this chapter, this constituency cross section gives greater visibility, political viability, and network strength to women's activism in Mexico. In the next chapter, we will see that this is much more restricted for women in El Paso/Ciudad Juárez, whose sociopolitical context has limited their activism to the U.S.-Mexico border.

But before going to the border comparison I provide in the next chapter, I should note several points. In a June 1995 General Assembly report, the women's NGOs represented there noted that one weakness in their efforts thus far was the lack of programs to train women leaders from among the NGO members of the State Coordinating Committee (Minutes 1995). Training this leadership is important because it increases participation by women from indigenous and popular sectors, in particular at regional and national levels. While the Michoacán women's NGO leadership recognized that many of the mission statements included commitments to put indigenous and poor women in leadership positions, they found that financial constraints limited their ability to develop training programs. But they reaffirmed their commitment to such programs as one way to begin turning those limitations around. In fact, as I stated in the introduction, Tomasa Sandoval of Mujeres Grupo Erandi eventually would be named national coordinator for indigenous women.

Several NGOs have recognized the leadership of indigenous and peasant communities. For example, members of the Asociación Ecologista Viva Natura noted that participation by women of the popular sector was very important to its efforts, particularly because their communities often were more directly impacted by Michoacán's ecological problems. For those reasons, Asociación Ecologista Viva Natura focused much of its teaching and training on empowering that sector of the population. Members of the Grupo Civil de Mujeres Gertrudis Bocanegra (Gertrudis Bocanegra Civilian Women's Group) noted that it is only by organizing in diverse political spaces, including, as they saw it, the work they were doing on the State Coordinating Committee, that they could bring about a broad-based women's emancipation. Others who formed the State Coordinating Committee expressed similar views, emphasizing working for all women across race and class lines.

SUMMARY

Notes from the Michoacán State Coordinating Committee meetings highlighted three points: (1) the relatively recent presence of women's NGOs in Michoacán, (2) the focus on poor and indigenous causes, and (3) the influence of those poor and indigenous women on the state and national women's NGOs. This influence is important to note because we do not want to argue that women's NGOs or their agendas were sparked by the World Conference on Women. What the UN "Toward Beijing" effort did was provide a propitious organizational moment when women's NGOs in communities like Michoacán could formalize the sharing of information and resources. The preparations for the conference allowed the women's NGOs to reaffirm their belief that issues of gender could not be separated from those of class and race and that this realization was part of their historical evolution as a movement. These NGOs solidified their relationships with one another by focusing on what was important to them as women with diverse backgrounds, particularly bringing to the women's movement ethnic and class struggles inseparable from their political articulations as a diverse women's movement.

The study of women's activism in Mexico shows that what was elusive to the movement in the 1970s, a convergence with women across class and race lines, began to take shape in the mid-1980s. Michoacán is a case in point. What is particularly important about the change is that women from a number of other movements, primarily poor urban, rural, peasant, and indigenous groups, made demands of what had been a predominantly academic and upper-class women's movement. This is important for students of social movements because poor people's movements throughout history have made demands of societies and sometimes of other social movements. The transformation of the Mexican women's movement underscores the fact that social movements often impact each other, intentionally and unintentionally.

Social movements in Mexico have converged on a number of political and social arenas. And as this study suggests, NGO networking was important for creating greater political opportunities. From the first Encuentro Nacional de Mujeres in Mexico City in 1980 to the networks that sprang from efforts to mobilize for the 1995 World Conference on Women in Beijing, women's NGOs in Mexico played a central role in shaping these opportunities. Women's groups in Mexico were able to integrate gender with class and race issues. Indigenous and nonindigenous women, working-class poor and privileged have changed the women's movement in Mexico with their activism at local, regional, and national levels. The World Conference on Women was a catalyst, enriching mobilization and dialogue among these women's NGOs, helping them to bring their concerns to international attention. The next chapter explores some of the same dynamics in the U.S.-Mexico border communities of El Paso and Ciudad Juárez by looking at how Latina activism was similar and how it differed from that in

Michoacán, even as women in the two regions shared a similar cultural and colonial heritage. For the greater El Paso/Ciudad Juárez communities, "Toward Beijing" had little to no effect in bringing women's NGOs together. By comparing these two communities, we learn how women's activism thrives despite such limitations. We also discover that border women share the global feminism articulated at the World Conference on Women.

CHAPTER TWO

Women's Activism in Greater El Paso / Ciudad Juárez

Women's NGOs in El Paso/Ciudad Juárez are strikingly similar to those in Michoacán. Yet mobilization strategies in the two areas differ in many ways. These differences are best understood by locating women's activism in local sociopolitical contexts. As we saw in the introduction, the present-day women's movement on the U.S.-Mexico border is not directly rooted in the Chicana/o movement or in the locally influential League of United Latin American Citizens (LULAC) — though these movements have a legacy in the region. Rather, U.S.-Mexico border politics shape women's NGO activism today, particularly in greater El Paso/Ciudad Juárez. In fact, only three NGO activists interviewed for this book articulated connections to the Chicana/o movement, and all three referred to it as part of their past activism. This chapter offers the basis for understanding women's activism on the border as it emerged in response to the arrival of transnational corporations and the continuing globalization of capitalism in the region. Globalization has similar effects on women activists in El Paso and Ciudad Juárez, particularly as they confront labor, health, and human rights issues.

This chapter compares and contrasts the themes and issues women's NGOs engage in El Paso/Ciudad Juárez to those in Michoacán and notes the very local nature of activism in El Paso/Ciudad Juárez. We will consider whether limiting networks and strategizing to local issues necessarily restricts Latina NGO activists' possibilities for success. The answer to this question is not obvious, because women's NGOs along this stretch of the border mobilize strategically. Sharon Navarro (2002: 193), for example, notes that "Even though La Mujer Obrera [The Woman Worker NGO in El Paso] knows that there exist some independent labor organizations in various Mexican cities along the border, the organizers have made a conscious decision to limit La Mujer Obrera's actions." María Antonia Flores, director of La Mujer Obrera, explained her group's relationship with organizations in Ciudad Juárez:

Our relationship is limited principally to supporting activities. Yes, we have activities, and we support [efforts in Ciudad Juárez], but we do not have a steady relationship. So, we do not work closely with the other side, because they have their own way of doing things and we have ours. They have their own [labor] rules to abide by in Juárez as it is in Mexico and then there are the U.S. [labor] laws. Therefore, it is something that is very different despite the fact that we have the same needs or sometimes worse.

Working within one country can make more sense if one considers the uphill battles with transnational corporations and separate government agencies; maneuvering within one legal system allows NGOs to use limited resources more efficiently, for one thing. But such situations can divide border NGOs. In fact, Staudt and Coronado (2002: 18) observe that labor and labor unions are "still steeped in national rather than cross-national solidarities and in 'justice' systems that do not affirm their interests above or at the level of business interests." And yet, NGOs do cooperate across the border, if only by supporting each other's work in protest rallies or events.

To understand the complex relationships between El Paso and Ciudad Juárez, one must understand that Latina organizing here is marked by histories and social contexts layered with human rights agendas that touch on broader border issues. For example, the murders of women in recent years along the U.S.-Mexico border has heightened awareness not only of violence against women but also of the plight of migrants, many of whom die of dehydration and other causes while trying to cross the desert. Women's NGOs on the U.S.-Mexico border have emerged to engage in this human rights arena, "constantly struggling to promote their agenda on both sides of the border because for many of them human rights issues transcend the border" (ibid.:

135). For these reasons, the intertwined histories of the cities of El Paso and Ciudad Juárez are the basis for understanding border women's NGOs.

Separated by a river but connected by a bridge, the lives of people on both sides are also linked economically and culturally. The river as divide is more meaningful to anti-immigration groups and Washington politicians than it is to local residents. Tim Padgett and Cathy Booth Thomas (2001) describe life in El Paso and Ciudad Juárez as "a tale of two cities in two countries — divided by an interstate highway (Interstate 10), the Rio Grande . . . , and an international border, but they are cities that share the benefits of trade and struggling with the pressures of growth." The two cities have a combined population of more than 2 million people (approximately 700,000 residents in El Paso and 1.5 million in Ciudad Juárez), making "the border region of El Paso, Texas, and Ciudad Juárez, Mexico, . . . the largest border community in the world" (ibid.). Essentially, "El Paso and Juárez are two halves of a single metropolis, sharing the same air, the same water, and the same future" (ibid.). As David Simcox (1993: 24) has noted, this has led some to question the terms commonly used to describe border life:

> The term "migration" is rejected as inapt by some area leaders, who emphasize that the twin cities of El Paso–Ciudad Juárez share common origins, culture and family connections and have economies that are increasingly interlinked. Under these circumstances, the international border separating them is regarded locally by some as "artificial," particularly among those who gain from an oversupply of labor and depressed wages.

And the intertwined histories of El Paso and Ciudad Juárez are rooted, as Alfredo Mirandé and Evangelina Enríquez argue (1979: 8), in "the parallels between the colonization of the American Southwest and the conquest of Mexico."

As Gloria Anzaldúa (1999: 25) put it, the U.S.-Mexican border became and continues to be "una herida abierta [an open wound] where the Third World grates against the first and bleeds." In this environment dispossessed peoples are most vulnerable. The legacy of the Mexican-American War and Mexico's defeat has shaped the U.S. perception of Mexico and the border region as a periphery economy. Under this economy Mexicans and Mexican

Americans are exploited as cheap labor and for material goods. *Maquiladoras*, "twin plant" factories, dot both sides of the border, characterizing its economy since the mid-1960s. U.S. companies have built these factories on the Mexican side, paying workers lower wages and contributing fewer taxes to the local economy than if the same factory were placed on the U.S. side of the border.

Maquiladoras, are a significant portion of the border economy, particularly in El Paso/Ciudad Juárez. "Ninety percent of the maquiladoras in Mexico are located along the U.S. border, and about one-third of these are located in Juárez," according to Ginger Thompson, who notes that there are more than 300 maquiladoras in Ciudad Juárez employing more than 226,000 Mexican workers, a significant increase from the twelve plants with 3,000 employees that existed at the time of the program's inception in 1965 (*New York Times*, February 11, 2001). The transnational border provides cheap labor for the twin plant factories, exposing workers on both sides to economic exploitation and the social conditions that result from it.

Initially the factory work that arrived was positive for local workers. Maria Antonia Flores of La Mujer Obrera described the change in attitude as business practices evolved in El Paso/Ciudad Juárez:

> In the period of the early sixties it was the time of the first factories to arrive in El Paso, the textile industry, with some magnificent benefits, good salaries, loans, money to be made. For those who had jobs in the factories it was nice. More importantly, there wasn't much abuse. Then the big companies started coming from about 1965 to 1970, . . . with the twin plants treaty. When that treaty passed, which [allowed companies] to create a factory in Juárez and one here, . . . to combine or coordinate the labor in Juárez with that of El Paso, and to provide growth for Juárez, so that there would be work there. Immediately . . . when the big companies came to the border . . . the door was open to the twin plant concept [and] the beginning of the increase in unemployment [for El Paso] and inconformity with labor [standards].

For transnational corporations border towns have become perfect locations to increase profit margins.

El Paso, like other border cities on the U.S. side, is dependent on its cross-border twin for labor that feeds plants in both countries. "*Maquiladoras* have attracted companion industries to El Paso that include warehousing and distribution, and capital-intensive manufacturing. According to the Greater El Paso Chamber of Commerce, Economic Development Division, the maquiladoras have generated more than twenty-five thousand jobs in indirect support industries, including retail sales, manufacturing support services, transportation, banking, and home building" (City of El Paso 2002: 11). Ironically, "as Juárez drives the economic boom in northern Mexico, El Paso, with persistent poverty, lags behind its sister city" (*New York Times*, February 11, 2001).

Women activists have responded by forming NGOs to address economic exploitation, its effect on living standards, housing, and myriad other social problems.

CONFRONTING LABOR ISSUES

Rubén García, who works at Annunciation House and spoke about it and Casa Peregrina (two shelters for illegal homeless immigrants, in El Paso and Ciudad Juárez, respectively) recalled:

> Because of the economic development of the border you have this incredible migration from the interior of Mexico to the border areas. You know the maquiladoras, the famous maquiladoras. When Annunciation House came into being, in 1978, the year before that the first maquila opened in Juárez, the RCA plant over at the Bermudez industrial park, and hired the first three thousand maquila workers. Well, almost twenty-two years later there's three hundred to four hundred maquiladoras, employing two hundred thousand plus people.

At first, as Flores of La Mujer Obrera noted above, the textile maquiladora factories that came to El Paso provided workers with "magnificent benefits, good salaries, loans, money to be made." Eventually all that changed, and worker dissatisfaction led to strikes — Flores recalled in particular the strike against the Farah Manufacturing Company in 1972. It has been studied by Laurie Coyle, Gail Hershatter, and Emily Honig (2001):

In May 1972, 4,000 garment workers at Farah Manufacturing Company in El Paso went out on strike for the right to be represented by a union. The strikers were virtually all Hispanic; 85 percent were women. Their labor action, which lasted until they won union representation in March 1974, grew to encompass a national boycott of Farah plants. Before the strike Farah was the second largest employer in El Paso. Low wages, minimal benefits, pressure to meet high production quotas, and tensions between workers and supervisors produced a dissatisfied work force.

La Mujer Obrera began as the women workers at Farah organized and learned how to form their own union. As Flores related, they realized that raising women's consciousness required educating them. This is why Flores joined the women's movement: "In reality, I didn't decide to join just to work in a movement. . . . When I came into it, it was 1986. We started an educational organization, an organization that worked toward developing women leaders precisely because we needed to get informed and get trained . . . about our rights, how to defend ourselves without always having to go out to get lawyers to defend us and even to speak for us." Flores realized just how marginalized women's voices were and was frustrated that the Farah leadership ignored her and others' complaints, exploiting their ignorance of how to form unions. But, Flores added, the women pushed on, complained, and formulated demands:

> And they ignored us. . . . So, the women with their own pride said, "We aren't ignorant. What we have to do is prepare ourselves better, learn about the law, our rights, and who we need to collaborate with, and then we'll be able to defend ourselves." . . . That was the first moment that opened the door to forming an organization for developing leadership, education, and training workers, . . . so that we could be able to mount our own defense. The organization came to be the Asociación de Trabajadores [Workers' Association], officially it was called El Centro del Obrero Fronterizo [The Center for the Border Worker], which had a small office. That was what was started in 1970.

Then around 1983–84 the Centro del Obrero Fronterizo developed a project on health as workers noticed that their own was suffering as a result of factory conditions. The Centro obtained funding to research the problem and out of that project came the center's spin-off group—the Programa de la Mujer Obrera (Program for the Woman Worker). This in turn led to the creation of the organization known today as La Mujer Obrera.

When Flores, its present executive officer, came to work for La Mujer Obrera in 1986, the group focused on educating women. According to Flores, developing women leaders was and continues to be its most important task: "We needed to be informed, trained, not with formal education, but with the kind of training that would teach us exactly what we needed to know to defend ourselves without always having to look for a lawyer to speak on our behalf. That was our challenge, to educate, train, and develop ourselves for our own defense."

Today, La Mujer Obrera focuses on unemployment as well as health. But the Centro del Obrero Fronterizo and La Mujer Obrera are not the only groups in the area to work on these issues. Patricia Monreal Molina of the Organización Popular Independiente (Popular Independent Organization, or OPI) in Ciudad Juárez talked about how she came to social activism and ultimately to the women's movement.

The thing is that since I was young I had experiences in working with women's groups from having been in pastoral work. I worked with *colonia* women, supporting them through parish work in what was at the time the base community movement. There I worked for a long time, working alongside women in more pastoral-type work. After that the same work opened opportunities from working with women in parishes to the colonia context. That was now a broader field that implied women working on a host of issues. That is how I came to work in OPI in 1987.

As Monreal Molina noted, the emergence of OPI coincided with the growth of the maquiladora industry:

This [the coming of the maquiladoras] had everything to do with the way city politics were oriented in favor of the installation of the maquiladoras. That is to say, the urban infrastructure, lights, and public services that were directed to areas where industrial parks were being constructed. That had a lot to do with the demands at that time, demands for basic public services, demand for water, drainage, electrification, and paved roads. At first, it seemed almost a privilege to be in areas where they were going to put a maquiladora. Instead it was local residents, not the maquiladoras, who were charged for putting in the infrastructure.

In response to the tension with local residents, federal monies were channeled to pay for the infrastructure to attract the factories. But Ciudad Juárez residents continued to be upset that no subsidies were earmarked for the colonias, which were straining the city's budget. And as maquiladoras grew more numerous so did the colonias, as new waves of migrants came to Ciudad Juárez for maquiladora jobs.

For NGOs like OPI, this made the focus of their protest "to denounce this type of politics which does not favor people's needs," as Monreal Molina put it. To raise awareness about what was happening in the colonias of Ciudad Juárez, she said,

> OPI was organized by a group of young people who brought their sociological backgrounds to make a statement about how to build people's lives with dignity. Some came from pastoral work, social work, and other backgrounds. But all wanted to open participation to address social issues. The colonias where many of us had started to work were very marked by PRI [Partido Revolucionario Institucional] leaders. In questioning corrupt political leaders, how they bribed people and played with people's demands, we came to promote a more authentic political organization or process.

Against that backdrop, OPI activists in 1987 started organizing, charging that government officials had laid out a red carpet for the maquiladoras at the expense of local residents. After tackling maquiladoras, OPI turned to other issues.

> At the time, the idea was to focus on issues that would bring the community together in a way that would encourage organizing from within the community, where people would come to empower themselves. At that time, we organized around ways to do communal buying. A lot of cooperatives were formed this way. All this type of "social action" generated a culture of self-help and solidarity in the community. That is a bit

how things evolved [for OPI]. And there were initiatives that were very, very local, including confronting price hikes. People would take over tortilla-making places so that prices would stay at a level they could afford. Then from confronting public services issues we went to other issues of basic needs.

In the end, OPI was able to show that the maquiladora industry created more social problems than it solved for El Paso and Ciudad Juárez.

Maquiladoras succeed in keeping wages low partly by pitting workers against those on the other side of the border. Flores of La Mujer Obrera and others noted that multinational companies undermine labor unions and demands for better pay by threatening to move operations over the border. Maquiladoras tend to employ young women, whom they can pay less because of these women's lack of experience. The women take maquiladora jobs in the hope they will provide reliable work and wages. The jobs also offer benefits, even though many women do not remain in a factory long enough to take advantage of them. And as Flores noted, factory management takes advantage of women who from birth are socialized to be submissive: "When one comes from Mexico with one's culture and ideology that shaped you one becomes submissive: one must obey, not lift one's voice, and instead aspire to be mother and wife. All of these things become a way to doubly abuse us," at home and at work. Studies show that low-skill and low-wage occupations exploit women of Mexican descent in border communities (Fernandez-Kelly 1984; Ruiz 1987; Lamphere 1993). Vicki Ruiz (1987) noted that during the 1980s El Paso was one of the poorest cities in the United States. Two decades later, little has changed. According to the U.S. Census Bureau (2000), median household income in El Paso in 2000 was $32,124, while for the rest of the state it was $39,927, and for the country as a whole it was $41,994. Furthermore, according to the 2004 U.S. Census Annual Supplement, nationwide the median income in 2003 for white men working full time was $37,579; for "Hispanic" men it was $23,462. "Hispanic" women lagged further behind with a median income of $20,222. White women earned $29,014. Moreover, for women in the El Paso/Ciudad Juárez area, work in the *maquilas* or as a maid often is seen as the only option for survival (Hondagneu-Sotelo 2001). But mass migration

to the region by Mexicans seeking jobs in the maquiladoras has over-
whelmed local social service organizations. Many who come to the border
find themselves not only unemployed but also joining the increasing homeless population in El Paso and Ciudad Juárez.

CONFRONTING HOMELESSNESS

As the number of the homeless has grown, NGOs providing shelter and
other services to migrants also have increased. Ruben García of Annunciation House, a Christian men's shelter, recalled that when it was founded in
1978, "there were no transitional living centers and there were no battered
women's shelters." García said that Annunciation came into existence because he and a few others committed to working with the border's poor.

> Little by little, by word of mouth, Annunciation House filled out. . . . It
> also so happened that coming into existence in 1978 coincided with the
> explosion that took place in Central America and the mass exodus of
> people from Guatemala, Nicaragua, El Salvador, Honduras [due to the
> civil wars]. And so, as these people made their way up to various kinds of
> borders, El Paso was one of the major crossing points for people. So, we
> found ourselves doing an immense amount of work with the refugees
> from Central America, along of course, with the people who have histor-
> ically crossed over from the interior of Mexico.

Annunciation House and Casa Peregrina were two shelters created in response to a housing crisis that neither El Paso nor Ciudad Juárez could
handle. Initially shelters for men, they came to serve women in various
ways, as migrants began to include single women, often with children, as
well as families with children. Estela, a migrant from Mexico in her sixties who attends the Centro Mujeres de Fe y Esperanza (Faith and Hope
Women's Center, which I discuss in more detail in chapter 3), said that
despite years of cleaning houses in El Paso, she finds herself homeless. Even
when women have family, she said, finding housing can be difficult.

> Right now, I do not have a home. I tell you this is how I live, like a
> feather in the air here and there and there. My daughters-in-law are good

women, but I feel that it is not the same [as when I was younger and could find more work cleaning houses]. My youngest boy got married and he made my house his house. He bought it in his name and stayed with everything. They have a little room for me and there I keep my clothes, but it is not my home.

Such narratives are common in El Paso and Ciudad Juárez, where shelters for women are in growing demand.

Annunciation House and Casa Peregrina were often mentioned by the NGOs associated I studied as organizations they turn to. The interviews particularly underscored the importance of these organizations for women. Women's shelters and other crisis centers emerged from the groundwork laid by Annunciation House and Casa Peregrina in bringing attention to homelessness in the region. These shelters have become part of the grassroots organizational network that Latinas and their families rely on in moments of crisis, particularly when families become homeless for economic reasons or as a result of domestic violence. La Posada, a battered women's shelter started by a group of Catholic nuns, has added to the social services provided by Annunciation House and Casa Peregrina (which also became a women's shelter). La Posada emerged at a time when Annunciation House was a shelter for men only. Sister Bernadette Habur, one of La Posada's founders, saw the need for the shelter precisely because little was available to women in the mid-1980s and because (as chapter 3 discusses in greater detail) her religious congregation saw the need to support these border community efforts.

Habur was working at Annunciation House in the mid-1980s and saw that women were going there, but there was no room for them. Habur tried to help by teaching survival skills.

I noticed what was happening to the women, so I started to do a little work with the women on seeing themselves as [people] who [needed to] value themselves as women. And so one day, I was talking to the director [Rubén García], and I said, "Don't you think you need another place?" and he said, "What is really needed is a shelter for women and children and not just a temporary thing, more of a transitional type of shelter where they could stay up to a year at least, in order to get back on their feet and see themselves as valuable people."

After learning how few social services the city of El Paso had to offer the growing population of immigrants, Habur opened La Posada in September 1986. The first house was on the North Loop, near the San Antonio Church.

La Posada initially focused on women who, according to a 1999 letter I received from Habur, "were terribly traumatized by their life experiences, a dysfunctional childhood and adult family life, abusive and violent relationships, abandonment, and thus experiencing abject homelessness." For these reasons "La Posada strives to provide a nurturing environment through which women can achieve a sense of self-worth and self-esteem, and become sufficiently independent and self-directed so as to be able to formulate and actualize long-term goals for [themselves] and [their] children." To turn the women's circumstances around, La Posada members and supporters believe that a set of basic goals have to be in place, one of which is to reverse the negative self-images many of the women bring to La Posada. A number come to La Posada because they are estranged from their families after having left Mexico on their own, but the majority come to the shelter because they are physically abused. Teresa said, "I have a lot of anger for all that I have suffered. It is not Mexico's fault, but I feel that I will never return to live there." Women give myriad reasons for why they leave home, including domestic violence, incest, the desire for economic independence from families, or the need to support families as primary breadwinners. Guadalupe, attending an event sponsored by the Centro de Fe y Esperanza, said that for her "there is no turning back. My brothers sometimes talk with me and say, 'Why don't you want to live here with us? It would be cheaper for you.' I won't go. What would I return to? I visit them, but I will never return." The YWCA in El Paso is another place that offers shelter to homeless women, often as referrals from area NGOs like the Centro de Fe y Esperanza.

The YWCA of El Paso del Norte Region, as it is referred to locally, has brought together women of diverse economic, ethnic, and social backgrounds since 1908. Florence Buchmueller, its programs administrator, described how the YWCA became involved with the more recent problem of homeless women.

The YWCA here learned that there were a lot of women sleeping in the branch parking lots of the Y, waiting for morning so they could take a shower and use the facility. This distressed the Y board, not just that this was happening, but why this was happening. . . . We're getting more and more large families, younger families, and nineteen-year-old girls with three children. . . . Our demographics are the same as the city, so we see 70 percent Hispanic.

The YWCA's informational flyers identify the isolation of homeless families as the primary difficulty that homeless women, with or without children, encounter in breaking the cycle of homelessness: "Their knowledge of how to build a supportive network is limited, therefore their resources are limited." If you add to this the recent arrivals' lack of English language skills and work or residency documents, the problem is compounded.

To respond to these needs, particularly as they affect women, the YWCA Transitional Living Center (YWCA-TLC) opened its doors to homeless women in 1993. As Buchmueller noted, YWCA-TLC is designed to bridge the gap between emergency shelter and permanent housing. Several strategies were adopted at the YWCA-TLC to help women find their way out of homelessness. One strategy was to offer training in managing money, parenting, nutrition, assertiveness, conflict management, and gaining employment. Others included programs for children and group and individual counseling "to improve the participants' abilities to meet the challenge of independent living" (YWCA-"Transitional Living" flyer). But the road to independence proves difficult for many border women. They find themselves limited by low levels of education and job training. "Low wages plague women on both sides of the border" (Staudt and Coronado 2002: 159). This is why NGOs like La Mujer Obrera, OPI, La Posada, and the YWCA focus on the economic limitations and emotional stress that border women experience in a world hostile to them. The women's movement on the U.S.-Mexico border is now centered on broad border issues that women's NGOs seek to address both by empowering border women and by advancing women's issues in the public sphere.

Through a series of joint programming efforts with a number of other local women's organizations, the staff of women's shelters and transitional housing attempt to improve the physical and emotional well-being of the women they serve. The hope, said Habur of La Posada, is that building self-esteem and independence will lead to employment. Since many of the women who arrive at these shelters come from abusive relationships, the first step to recovery is removing the pressures that often force women to return to abusive relationships. Prominent among these is financial dependency. La Posada thus provides financial assistance, information, and training for women so they can establish their own homes, provide for their children, and take control of their future. To empower women to gain independence, La Posada uses counseling and training on health, nutrition, domestic violence, and other issues to educate women about their options. Some of the women who have succeeded return to support the women's groups that helped them, becoming community activists.

Because of its success since 1986, Habur noted, La Posada has enjoyed a lot of support from other organizations:

We have sent some of our families to the Salvation Army transitional living center. If need be, we could recommend them also to the YWCA transitional living center. We also belong to the Coalition for the Homeless. We all sort of really work together, and the Y has just been very good; they periodically come in and give a whole day parenting session to our women, and this really comes out of [the YWCA's] Project Redirection. So we're always working together. Our closest ties happen to be with the Salvation Army.

This type of collaboration has become an extension of a "cross-border activity common in the health care arena" (Staudt and Coronado 2002: 156). These relational ties among the various local NGOs offer women expanded resources more efficiently. Once an NGO is in a network, using referrals becomes key to both providing expanded services for women and to reinforcing the NGO's place in the network, no matter its size or budget. As Habur noted, the network is often key to how people find out about La Posada:

Oh, we're pretty well known, but we get our references. Like today we had a call from the Shelter for Battered Women: they have a woman that needs more time [to stay than the shelter can offer], as with the Salvation Army, the Rescue Mission, and the hospital. You'd be amazed at how many calls we get from the hospital, clinics, even individual people who know us, or people who have been with us and met up with a woman that was in really bad shape.

The referrals often include assessments of women's needs and the services that could help them. One of the biggest challenges domestic violence centers face is the low self-esteem of many victims of domestic violence, which, Habur noted, is "one of the main reasons women return to their abusers." Developing strategies to improve self-esteem has become a priority for women's shelters. For Habur and other staff of shelters confronting domestic violence as a social problem requires not just creating shelters but also creating spaces that empower women more broadly. These are the challenges that grassroots women's NGOs on the U.S.-Mexico border and Mexico bring to feminism. As Chandra Talpade Mohanty (2003: 229) suggests, third world women's communities are taking on these issues and pushing feminist thinking "to be attentive to the micropolitics of everyday life as well as to the larger processes that recolonize the culture and identities of people across the globe." NGOs like La Posada, La Mujer Obrera, OPI, and others highlighted in this book provide more than services.

From the perspectives of the women who come to work in the NGOs, women need spaces to tell their stories if they are to be empowered. Newsletters put together by participants in activities sponsored by women's NGOs show that women feel empowered by these organizations, thus revealing strategies for developing feminist futures. The Centro Mujeres de Fe y Esperanza 1997 winter newsletter *Esperanza* noted that women gather at the center to find safe spaces where they can share, where their voices are respected and where they make a difference, where they strengthen and support one another, and where they discover their gifts, especially of leadership — to be more effective in their families and communities. The newsletter advertised that "We gather to learn, to help one another through difficult times and celebrate special events in our own lives and the life of the community." Other newsletters reveal that, for many women, these NGOs are the first place they have felt empowered to look at gender relations as a source of their pain. The winter 1995 *Esperanza* newsletter noted how important it was for women to recognize that "at home we can initiate a focus on gender equality that . . . implies a sharing of power between men and women that is done in a more just manner." Facing relationships at home thus means confronting one's past and how it is connected to women's position in patriarchal relationships, recognizing that there are other models for creating family.

The narratives show that women's NGOs not only empower women but help them tap into their own "feminist" cultures of resistance against domestic violence by allowing them to understand its root causes. If we extend to Latinas what Patricia Hill Collins argues about the empowerment process of African American women, Latina NGOs in the United States and Mexico become the spaces where a process is created in which women can acquire a voice. Collins (2000: 119) illustrates her point with the experience of Celie in Alice Walker's *The Color Purple*: "the act of acquiring a voice through writing, of breaking the silence with language, eventually moves her to the action of talking with others." This approach shows us how Latinas have come to stand against the dominant ideology promulgated in patriarchal societal institutions — those rooted in the Latino community as well as those of other dominant societies such as that of the United States. On this point, border women today stress the struggle that women in the El Paso/Ciudad Juárez region have been waging for a long time. Enriqueta Longauex y Vásquez (n.d.), an El Paso activist, reflected after attending a La Raza conference in Colorado in the 1970s that "there are many things she [a woman] must do. She must: (1) Find a way to feed and clothe the family; (2) Find housing; (3) Find employment; (4) Provide child care, including (5) Finding some kind of social outlet and friendship" for her survival. Since the 1970s, the border has remained a region where people of Mexican descent are isolated from family and other social networks that conspire to weaken their social, economic, and political position.

"The challenges that women face in the border region are many. The issues they encounter run the gamut from the legal, criminal, and medical to work-related concerns" (Staudt and Coronado 2002: 156). María de Jesús Gringas Aguirre of the Centro Mujeres Tonantzín in Ciudad Juárez noted the process that leads some border women to become involved in illegal activities: "Much of it is a consequence of the economic situation, because of low wages and the overall needs they have given the situation they find themselves in. They come [to the border] looking for a better life and on not finding it they get involved in selling drugs or their bodies." Women's NGOs are rare places that give women a context in which to reconnect to support systems.

Cooperation between NGOs in Ciudad Juárez and in El Paso has become increasingly important as both communities share information, personnel, and other resources to make addressing social needs more manageable. For example, the Centro para el Desarrollo Integral de la Mujer, A.C. (Center for the Integral Development of Women Inc., or CEDIMAC), in Ciudad Juárez, confronts similar issues of violence against women as La Posada and thus provides similar services. But CEDIMAC does so primarily by offering legal advice and counseling. As the founder and director of CEDIMAC, Dolores Leony, noted, her group provides "all the moral support that we can offer, sometimes by raising money to help women return to their parents . . . — it is the rare case, but we do it."

Leony started CEDIMAC with a group of women who became disillusioned about fighting the Immigration and Naturalization Service and the Border Patrol after losing court battles in what they saw as clear cases of abuses against border crossers. They found that far too few agents who are accused of abuse are disciplined. In 1992, after years working with the Border Coalition, which focuses on human rights violations on the U.S.-Mexico border, Leony helped form CEDIMAC. The journey to create CEDIMAC for Leony came out of her own experience of border abuse, despite being a woman of relative privilege. This led her to work with the League for Immigration and Border Rights Education (LIBRE), which was part of the Border Coalition.

> After an experience I had had on the bridge [the Santa Fe bridge that links Ciudad Juárez to El Paso] with a customs official who physically mistreated me more than anything, and verbally as well, I decided to work with them [LIBRE]. Back then I worked documenting abuse cases on the part of American authorities, not just on the undocumented, but also with people who had their papers who suffered from the violence, aggression, and abuses from the authorities. That included customs, border patrol, INS agencies, and even the El Paso police. We documented a lot.

For Leony, her experience with border officials led her to observe similarities between abuse on the border and domestic violence: "In both instances the issue is about power and its abuses."

The lessons Leony learned in border work brought her to link the violence affecting women with the little recourse they have to confront their attackers. After activist work on the border it was easy for Leony to move to working against domestic violence. She and her colleagues at CEDIMAC joined the fight against sexual and domestic violence. To tackle violence against women and its physical and mental effects, CEDIMAC focused on providing free psychological, legal, and emotional support to victims. Leony and others who support the work of CEDIMAC see these services as a way to support women in crisis and at the same time to mobilize and raise consciousness about sexual and domestic abuse in other venues.

Sometimes there are meetings that bring women's groups together from Chihuahua [the state in which Ciudad Juárez is located]; we have attended some of these, including the Primer Encuentro Estatal de Mujeres de Chihuahua [First State Meeting of Women of Chihuahua], and then we formed part of the organizing committee of the Second State meeting. . . . We have reached out to others on other occasions as well because we would like to focus on broader issues that touch women's lives. But because of limited resources we focus more directly on violence against women. We consider the violence more urgent to attend to.

Leony made it clear that while CEDIMAC is constrained by limited funds, issue-oriented mobilizing links CEDIMAC to other women's organizations. For example, raising women's awareness and empowering them through health education often has become the basis for connecting with other NGOs. Leony noted in particular her links with La Posada and the Centro Mujeres de Fe y Esperanza in El Paso.

CONFRONTING HEALTH AND EDUCATION

These organizations ask border women about the links between their health and broader women's issues. Establishing this linkage, Habur of La Posada noted, begins with basic questions:

We interview women about their health, if they've ever had tuberculosis, or diabetes. We ask if they've been tested for sexually transmitted diseases, and for HIV. We don't ask results but we ask if they've been tested; if not, we encourage them to be tested. [We ask] if they've ever been hospitalized, you know, other than for the birth of their children, the basics. . . . Another thing that you will pick up on as you're talking with the woman is her emotional state, and that's one of our reasons for the interview, just to pick up on how they feel, you know, how depressed they are, and many are very depressed. The issue of suicide often comes up and is a major concern for La Posada.

These questions help link abuse against women and the social institutions that support it. They lead women to reject patriarchal marriages, which by definition reinforce women's subordination and sometimes abuse them. Graciela[1] of El Paso, who is active in the Centro Mujeres de Fe y Esperanza, described her commitment to her relationship with her husband: "As they say about marriage, it is a sacred thing. So for me that was my vision when I got married in white. It was sacred and I got married in the [Catholic] church. For me it was something where I was disposed to pass through, for good or for bad." But after years in a physically and emotionally abusive marriage, Graciela said, there came a turning point for her. After her husband beat and raped her, doing things "that you wouldn't do even to an animal," she went to a priest for advice and his blessing to leave her husband. Instead of supporting her, the priest advised her to go back to her husband and "work things out."

Graciela not only decided to leave her husband, she turned to local women's NGOs for support and in the process came to question the church's response to her pain.

How can a church, an organization, or society, judge me because of what it teaches us? I say what's better: that I as a woman, because of what society says that because I was married in white, in a church, that I had to "work with him" [her ex-husband] despite being abused for ten years? What is better: to have continued to put up with it because of the veil and crown, and for the church, to work with him?

Graciela described how she has come to heal and learn to love herself and her body and has discovered a newly empowered spirituality through her participation and activism in the Centro Mujeres de Fe y Esperanza. Her case illustrates that questioning can draw women into women's NGO programs. A 1999 El Centro Mujeres de Fe y Esperanza empowerment program flyer highlighted that through creative and interactive processes women explore themes such as "What is important in my life? What are my values? What happens when two people have values that conflict? How can conflicts be resolved? Am I controlled by things that happened to me in the past? How can I let go of them? What is power? Do I have power to change situations in which I find myself?" For many women's NGOs, these questions become critical in raising women's consciousness of the fact that, globally, violence against women is directly linked to societal beliefs and practices that subordinate women.

María Antonia Flores of La Mujer Obrera noted that Latinas have to confront machismo in Latino communities, including in local organizing. For many of the border women's NGOs, that was the challenge.

So we had to educate, prepare, and develop ourselves for our own defense, to be our own defenders, produce our own leadership, because the corruption that existed in the factories even where there were unions was machismo, the abuse against women. It was the lack of respect for women. . . . Consequently, we worked on becoming our own defenders to learn how to defend ourselves to put into action our own struggle to survive without always having to be under someone telling us do this, that, or don't do that. . . . In that way our organization moved to create our own women's leadership, pushing women's development, preparing and educating ourselves by raising awareness about the system in which we live. It is not just about survival, meaning if you work you are realized. That is not true. . . . We work to prepare ourselves to fight economically, politically, and socially.

Flores went on to clarify what she and others of La Mujer Obrera mean by the three-pronged approach — economic, political, and social — they take to problems that feed violence against women. "You have rights as a human being to demand change" on these fronts. The sheer number of women being murdered, sexually and physically assaulted, and economically exploited on the border today underscores how much women's NGOs have to confront. The demands can be overwhelming. But women's networks are strengthened when women like Leony are invited to collaborate with others through workshops and serving on the boards of other women's NGOs, as she does for the Centro Mujeres de Fe y Esperanza in El Paso. "I don't know how they came to hear about CEDIMAC," Leony said, "but it was they [Centro Mujeres de Fe y Esperanza] who took the initiative to find CEDIMAC. For that I am very grateful, because the funds, most of the funds that CEDIMAC has received have come thanks to their [Centro de Fe y Esperanza's] linkages with foundations."

The relationship between CEDIMAC and the Centro de Fe y Esperanza goes back to 1996 and further illustrates the different ways in which women's NGOs in El Paso are linked for mutual support. CEDIMAC's tie to the Centro de Fe y Esparanza not only benefits both groups, it exemplifies a pattern in Latina activism in the United States and Mexico. The reasons for the pattern are best understood by listening to women like Erlinda Robles, a Mexican American activist in East Los Angeles interviewed for Mary Pardo's (1998b: 267) study. Robles observed that linkages are made even with unlikely partners: "We had nuns who were ahead of their time . . . and a lot of mothers would go to them for counseling." Faith-based groups "serve as a bridge to local secular institutions" (ibid.). In El Paso and Ciudad Juárez faith-based women's NGOs came to play important roles and held important positions in the Latina NGO network.

As Leony noted, the networks allow for the exchange of information: "They [the Centro] send us informational pamphlets every month and we make this information available to every woman who comes here." These exchanges help CEDIMAC to meet its objectives and are symbiotic, with CEDIMAC providing services to other women's organizations, often extending the work to include broader human rights issues. The women's movement owes this quality of its activism to the work of grassroots women's organizations, which have developed the movement's transnational potential. And in becoming transnational, the movement embraces new approaches to family issues, since, as a number of the women's NGOs see it, patriarchal power manifests itself throughout the family structure. One group that uses this approach is Bienestar Familiar (Family Well-Being), a spin-off organization of the Centro Mujeres de Fe y Esperanza. Imelda García, a cofounder of the group, noted how activism around family and health is nurtured in the relationship between the Centro Mujeres de Fe y Esperanza and Bienestar Familiar:

> About two years ago, Lorenza Zuniga and [others of the El Paso Border Health Office] approached me that they had dreams about doing something special and could I get together with them to look at things. I said sure and so we met and then I came back and talked to Jean [Duran] and Ida [Berresheim] [from the Centro Mujeres de Fe y Esperanza] about it and then we brought in Sally Andrade from UTEP [the University of Texas at El Paso]. . . . And we all started working on funding. At the same time, one of the women, Rosie Higgs at Wayne Wright Elementary, who had led one of our programs at her clinic in the Northeast called . . . [one of the local] foundations. . . . So we got El Paso North Foundation [to support a project]. And so it's like everything fell together and we developed a grant for a healthy communities project.

From that initial exchange, a project was created in 1997 to promote healthy families and communities that would empower women.

García noted that the basic principles, objectives, and goals of Bienestar Familiar were "to give voice to the community and to work with the community to better their health and health not just related to blood pressure and whatever. . . . It's not just geared toward the traditional limits of health, but basically to empower community. It's what we're all about." At the time of the interview with García, Bienestar Familiar was working primarily in an El Paso community known as Socorro.

> Basically we started out . . . with a vision of what a healthy Socorro would be like. . . . They [residents of Socorro] wanted to work on education and the environment the first year. What they came up with was a plan to clean five neighborhoods, offering paint to people . . . to paint the outside [at first] of five homes for people that were really in need. . . . Then with the education part we developed more people as

community workers, . . . just to begin to give people a voice. . . . We tried to train at least six people to go out and organize in the community and try to bring [neighbors] to meetings and things like that. . . . I think that the big thing . . . the first year was to try to develop a group of people that could serve as a council.

Bienestar Familiar then created a number of community programs. Since the group's interest was in family health, the first programs centered on workshops about family issues.

One year Bienestar Familiar and the Socorro community brought in Jerry Tello, a well-known Latino family consultant, to talk about his curriculum Cara y Corazón (Face and Heart). One program that Tello developed, Hombre Noble (Noble Man), was of particular interest to the women of Bienestar Familiar because it sought to help men reduce domestic violence. As García put it:

The women wanted something for the men, because a lot of them go back to their husbands. They may leave them for a while, but they wind up going back and they said, "Well, there's nothing." And, so part of what we wanted to do was to do something to start getting men involved and so Mr. Tello [came] . . . to do a two-day retreat to train the first group of men. Training them as elders and dealing with their issues and talking to them and why it's important to get men involved. That was something . . . we wanted to do.

García credited the Paso del Norte Health Foundation with helping to fund these programs and with providing other opportunities that contributed to Bienestar Familiar's initial success: "They opened a lot doors for Bienestar Familiar."

For Bienestar Familiar as for other women's NGOs in the region, success and the ability to develop community projects depended on relationships with other local organizations and agencies. García measures the success of Bienestar Familiar by noting that it attracts women who are "nontraditional in approaching people." By that she means that a lot of agencies come forward to support community projects because of the personal relationships women nurture in community work.

And that's ultimately how everything gets done. We were able to establish relationships with a community college. We were able to establish relationships with the different programs with the Socorro school district. We tried to bring older families into our council, people that had been there forever and ever, some of the original families from the area. And that has been very difficult, because there seems to be a split between the recent immigrants and people that have been there a long time.

Pardo (1998b: 276) notes that this conflict between recent arrivals and longer-established Mexican American residents is found in a number of Mexican migration studies: "One of the few community studies of immigrant and native-born social interaction suggests that immigrants and native-born Mexican Americans hold critical perceptions of each other." In fact, when you look at the El Paso and Ciudad Juárez communities outside the context of NGO activism, it is not always a story of collaboration and partnership. Sociologist Pablo Vila (2000: viii) notes that when you take into account how they articulate their border identities, "the real lives of Juarenses and El Pasoans are forged out of the complex articulation of racial, ethnic, regional, national, religious, gender, age, and class identity categories (among others)." And yet despite the conflicts that erupt from time to time, particularly on how to handle illegal immigration, NGOs on opposite sides of the border do work together. Research shows that despite difficulties, cross-border organizing and transnational support for NGO activism is taking place (Staudt and Coronado 2002). The greater challenge for NGOs is not so much the immigration issue, but rather finding funding to promote their community projects.

For example, much of the funding for Bienestar Familiar comes from local organizations, with some provided by the Catholic sisters whose religious orders support its work. García estimated the Catholic sisters' support at three thousand dollars. But the bulk of the financial support came initially from the El Paso North Foundation in the form of a three-year grant. But like many of NGOs, Bienestar Familiar must constantly search for funding. "We're getting into our final year [of the El Paso North Foundation three-year grant]," García noted in 1999, "and so what I'm trying to do right now is to diversify our funding sources so we can continue and grow."

I discuss the problem of funding and its threat to the survival of many women's NGOs in chapter 4. Although many NGOs survive because of their relationships with other groups, we should note that the independence and effectiveness of NGOs like Bienestar Familiar does depend on foundation monies. As we will see in chapter 4, this dependence can influence the content of workshops, programming, and other NGO initiatives. The struggle for funding sometimes creates conflict between salaried and nonsalaried activists.

Women living on opposite sides of the Rio Grande are linked by issues confronting both communities. María de Jesús Gringas Aguirre of the Centro Mujeres Tonantzín in El Paso underscored the importance of these relationships and the overlapping that takes place among the area NGOs. In identifying the projects that the Centro Mujeres Tonantzín supports, Gringas Aguirre noted its emphasis on legal, pastoral, family, and health issues similar to those confronted by other area women's NGOs. Since opening its doors in September 1997, the Centro Mujeres Tonantzín has directed most of its workshops and activities to colonias in the Ciudad Juárez area. It serves mostly "the marginalized women," Gringas Aguirre said, "the oppressed women, the women most in need—the poor. . . . We dedicate our efforts to women living in the peripheral parishes [colonia Catholic parishes] and with the traumatized women in prison. Those in prison are the poor, poor, poor. Our work takes place in parish groups, with prostitutes and drug addicts." Working with the poorest of the poor brought Gringas Aguirre, a Catholic Sister of the Incarnate Word, to the women's movement and led her to help open the Centro Mujeres Tonantzín: "I believe that among the most oppressed, among the most in need, are women, especially the poor, marginalized, mistreated, and humiliated. I feel a great calling to limit my work to working with these women. We need to recuperate our dignity together, our place in society, our families, and our churches." Furthermore, she sees a connection between herself a Catholic nun, a member of a patriarchal church, where she is a marginal figure as a woman, with women who are marginalized in their homes and in the society that the Catholic Church supports in its teachings.

As Gringas Aguirre noted, many colonia women "come to the Centro Tonantzín for reasons that have to do with women's issues, domestic violence, and other kinds of violence, because a number of migrant women find themselves forced into prostitution in order to feed their children." From prostitution, many of the women find their way to drugs and the associated cycle of violence. No single issue has elevated the notion of sisterhood among border women's NGOs more than violence against women. Several women's NGOs on the border were formed specifically to work with battered women and victims of sexual violence.

CONFRONTING VIOLENCE AGAINST WOMEN

On the El Paso side of the Rio Grande, the Battered Women's Shelter is probably the organization with the highest visibility. Rosemary Combs, the shelter's executive director, recalled that it began when the Jewish Women's Council of El Paso started talking about domestic violence. "They realized and recognized it was a problem here, and they established and have supported the Battered Women's Shelter ever since." One of the most influential women in this group was Ruth Schwartz Zork, who worked for more than fifty years on El Paso community projects (*El Paso Times*, December 26, 1993) and raised eight hundred thousand dollars to build the Brown Street YWCA downtown. The El Paso Shelter for Battered Women now serves three counties, and it provided more than thirty-two thousand shelter days in 1998, making it the largest such facility in Texas (*El Paso Times*, October 14, 1999).

These shelters have become critical to the mobilization against the disappearance of over four hundred women in the Juárez desert and the murder of three hundred more since 1993 (Marchand 2004: 90). Local residents and women's organizations have mobilized not just to catch the perpetrators but to bring broader meaning to the victimization of border women. Violence against border women reveals a deeper interplay between economic exploitation, racism, and sexism. The interplay cannot be explained simply by looking at globalization processes and their effects. In her analysis of reporting on the murders, the women's studies scholar Melissa Wright (1999: 456) observed that "onlookers try to determine if the murder victims were prostitutes, dutiful daughters, dedicated mothers, women leading 'double lives,' or responsible workers," questioning, in short, whether the murdered women were "good girls." For Rosa Linda Fregoso (2003: 19), a "more nuanced understanding of sexual violence in Juárez identifies the multiple sites where women experience violence, within domestic and public spaces that are local and national as well as global and transnational. . . . this leads us to another way in which globalism is complicitous with the state." These analyses of the murders help us understand why local women's groups call for government intervention, more women's shelters, and rally women around the root causes of violence against them. NGOs that emerged in Ciudad Juárez after the murders began, together with previously established groups, highlighted these and other instances of violence against women as a symptoms of larger problems.

For Monreal Molina of OPI, the efforts to organize women's groups in Ciudad Juárez around the murder and disappearance of women in the desert constituted a "demand that here in Juárez we have an agency for sexual crimes which had not existed." Simply put, the murders galvanized the women's movement on the border. OPI and other local women's groups in the umbrella coalition known as the Border Women's Project used the annual International Women's Day (March 8) to bring attention to the murders and to broader women's issues. As Donna Kustusch of the Ciudad Juárez office of Centro Mujeres de Fe y Esperanza put it, the effort is designed to "focus on issues that are intrinsic to the border . . . as well as [bring] attention to the women's murders and disappearances across national borders." Anne Marie Mackler, the editor of *Frontera NorteSur*, noted that the majority of the victims are young women, often workers at the mostly American-owned maquiladoras. But she also observed that, "as a region, this is really a concern to all of us. It's not just a concern to people on the other side of the border. It affects everybody" (*El Paso Times*, September 26, 1999). Linking the murders to broader border and women's issues challenges the notion that social life can be divided into public and private realms.

Perhaps Pardo (1998b: 297) said it best when she wrote, "When feminists coined the slogan 'the personal is political,' they expressed the relation between the private sphere of family and the public sphere of community." Families who have lost loved ones to violence in the Juárez desert are met with NGOs who see their cause as a community crisis. In making these connections grassroots women have transformed the women's movement. Grassroots women's organizations show that while the personal and political may be "conceptualized as separate spheres by some, the work women do to mediate between family and community institutions clearly reveals how the two are interconnected" (ibid.). This is why, for border Latinas and for non-Latinas who have joined them in the struggle for women's rights, violence against women is not just a woman's personal matter; it is a matter for all women. Taking this position also centers women's experiences in global contexts. If women's issues were simply viewed as personal matters, it would cripple our capacity to analyze women's status in the family and in civil society, impeding our broader understanding of the root causes of inequality and victimization.

BUILDING SELF-ESTEEM AND EMPOWERING WOMEN

As Monreal Molina of OPI observed, women's groups often seek to empower women as community organizers. The process begins with the women themselves. "In other words," she said, "colonia women are the ones who organize their communities, who help to bring water and drainage to their communities, and are the main movers to make meetings happen." Such activism allows border women to then focus on themselves, on their particular issues as women, and their victimization and marginal status as women. Many start with family and children's concerns, a set of issues that many women's NGOs now include in their focus, as Monreal Molina noted.

> With the women we started by generating projects specifically focused on their children. For example, with the support of the organization [OPI], but promoted by the women themselves, we now have a whole area focused on attention to children, from daycare, preschool, to a whole center dedicated to a system of care for children. All these programs that we are now telling you about are programs dedicated to caring for children in the marginal zones [the colonias]. All this was a product of many years of working to organize and was generated by the women themselves as part of their empowering themselves to lead and direct projects they themselves wanted to develop. Now every single one

of those projects is put together with women trained with skills for all this . . . that now also has a reflective component to it [for raising gender consciousness].

These critical reflections are used to call other women to community organizing. When a woman comes to a point where she wants to realize her political potential, Monreal Molina said, "she asks why she is the only one who is concerned for her children." This is important because, as Lilia Rodríguez (1994: 35) notes, coming to understand why "women and men perform different roles, have distinct needs, social responsibilities, expectations and power, and are socialized in different ways" is the road to gender consciousness.

Coming to "this realization," said Monreal Molina, "helped us understand that we could not continue reinforcing the same [gendered expectations] in our work":

If there were many women who were happy to have learned [skills in the process of doing community work], including valuing the fact that they were not buried in their homes and that there were these other spaces where [they] could be and could participate in, a place where [their] self-esteem could develop . . . there was still the feeling that we needed to do deeper reflecting on women, their condition, and situation [at home, in the community, and larger society]. That's how we started to do other types of work, perhaps less activist but more to support women in learning to think for themselves about their own condition and to think about their own strategies for change. So we started a series of activities to define spaces for developing this [gender consciousness] in women and to support them in the process. The rest continues to move forward as women continue to mobilize, to push for change, but we are doing so while at the same time trying to promote the right environment for women to advance their own causes.

Monreal Molina also noted that women in OPI network with mothers who are educators. The strategy here is to promote education for themselves and their children.

With this strategy women are pushing men to work with them because as

Monreal Molina puts it, "their children's education is not just women's responsibility, but a responsibility that belongs to couples as equal partners. . . . We are encouraging women to see themselves as potential social actors with the sense that they are capable of many things, bettering their surroundings and at the same time bettering themselves." These approaches work because "women have become leaders of coordinating committees; they are making demands, taking action by pushing public issues, and are creating alliances with other women's groups." Pardo (1998b: 298) describes the evolution of this important process in Latina activism:

Through unpaid community work, women gain skills and experience fundraising, organizing neighborhood groups, negotiating with authority figures such as priests, husbands, and city officials, and managing households and family. The gendered nature of women's community work informs the strategies they use to create neighborhood networks that significantly improve the quality of life in their communities.

. . . It is really difficult to do this work, because many border women live at subsistence levels and we have adopted a way of doing things in a way where everyone can have a voice. It has been very enriching, because coming together has allowed us to feel very closely the plight of women, particularly in the poor and colonia sectors of society.

Monreal Molina stressed that forming alliances provides opportunities for the women's movement. Nowhere is this embrace more powerful than when women reach out to other women's groups.

One group OPI works with is the Centro Mujeres de Fe y Esperanza, which has locales in both Ciudad Juárez and El Paso. For many women in both cities, the Centro offers a safe space to gather and speak about issues important to them. The newsletters of Centro Mujeres de Fe y Esperanza and other women's centers provide outlets for women to share their journey stories and learn the importance of women's organizations. In the fall *Esperanza* 1996 newsletter, a recent woman arrival to the border tells of her struggle in the United States and then underscores the importance of narratives like her own: "Rarely do we catch a glimpse into the daily life of immigrants struggling to provide for their families. . . . Centro Mujeres gives us that much needed glimpse." Other newsletters highlighted the importance women place in creating safe spaces in NGOs like the Centro for sharing their stories. Specifically, the fall 1996 *Esperanza* highlighted how women of the Lower Valley, the rural eastern outskirts of El Paso, open their homes for the Centro Mujeres de Fe y Esperanza eight-week personal growth program or for a morning of retreat, each session beginning with coffee and rolls and comfortable sharing. The time women spend together is highlighted as empowering.

> Women gather to find safe spaces where they can share, where their voices are respected and where they make a difference, where they strengthen and support one another and where they discover their gifts, especially of leadership — to be more effective in their families and communities. The 1997 winter *Esperanza* newsletter underscored that women gather to learn, to help one another through difficult times and celebrate special events in their own lives and the life of the community.

These moments organized for sharing become the seedbeds for women's gender consciousness building. A 1998 Centro event flyer noted that "the idea behind gathering is to form a group of border women who meet to exchange information, ideas, and support" for one another to bring about change. According to the 1995 winter *Esperanza* newsletter, women at these events gather and gain the strength to demand that "at home we initiate a focus on gender equality that . . . implies a sharing of power between men and women that is done in a more just manner."

What makes the Centro unlike the more typical NGOs in El Paso and Ciudad Juárez is that much of its work was started and continues to be supported by Catholic sisters. I touched on this link in the introduction and will further detail it in chapter 3. I note it here to underscore the fact that border community work engages diverse constituencies, particularly as these constituencies bring resources to border NGOs. For example, Kustusch, who works on the Ciudad Juárez side for the Centro, runs self-esteem workshops. "The women just take to the programs very, very much," and "it seems to address things that they didn't even know they were struggling with in terms of their own self-esteem or who's making decisions for them and what their own capacities and gifts are for making their own decisions." Echoing the sentiment, Habur of La Posada noted,

Our whole program is really designed, we hope, to help the women liberate themselves. . . . Just as an example, one of our women a couple of years ago got her own place, and she left an abusive situation; she got her home, and she did this all on her own; she got her lawyer, with a little help. When she got her home, she just got up and moved. And her husband had to deal with that, and he would come to pick up the kids once a week and take them out for a pizza or something. . . . He [the husband] said to me, one day when he came to see me to talk about things, after she left, he said, "You know, she's just not the same anymore." I . . . said, "Well, thank goodness," you know, because she had enough get-up-and-go to change her life around.

Women are able to go to school, gain job skills, learn how to run their own financial affairs — all part of a strategy to help them become independent and feel free and empowered to leave abusive relationships. As Habur put it, the goal is to have "none of the women who leave from here leave without having a place to live, and the possibility of earning their way," and at the same time leave with the tools necessary to shape their own destinies.

Another faith-based NGO that supports women developing economic independence is the Women's Intercultural Center, which was started in 1993 by a few Latinas and three Catholic Sisters of Mercy. The center is located near El Paso in Anthony, a small town that straddles the border between New Mexico and Texas. According to the group's flyer: "The mission of the Women's Intercultural Center is to provide a place where the women of the Mesilla Valley can learn and work together to develop their own economic, social and spiritual potential" (Women's Intercultural Center Mission, 1999). To realize this goal, in March 1994, several women from the Women's Intercultural Center, with the help of the Federación Mexicana de Asociaciones Privadas (Mexican Federation of Private Associations, or FEMAP) of Ciudad Juárez formed a small community bank with the goal of teaching people how to start a small businesses. While the Women's Intercultural Center is located outside El Paso and Ciudad Juárez, FEMAP has provided a base for links between the cities to address shared economic needs and public health concerns. Among several community projects FEMAP funded was Seeds across the Border, which used the community bank model to provide low interest loans. On May 1, 1995, the Women's Intercultural Center used this model to create the Mujeres Unidas (Women United) Cooperative, which now operates as a spin-off of the Women's Intercultural Center. Mujeres Unidas' goal, as highlighted in its flyers, is to teach local women how to run successful small businesses as well as skills to make them more employable. Programs helped women develop products they could sell locally. In the process, they learned about finance, business planning, and marketing. In 1997, the Mujeres Unidas cooperative was recognized by the New Mexico Community Foundation and honored by a "Community Luminaria" award. In 1999, Mujeres Unidas began to run the cooperative out of a storefront in downtown Anthony. Despite the group's successes, Mujeres Unidas has had to shift its carpentry work to sewing, given the difficulty and expense of stripping furniture. It continues to sell its products locally and has expanded sales to the World Wide Web.

NGOs are vulnerable to a host of limits on their effectiveness, including their dependency on funding. Other limitations include the difficulty women confront as they challenge traditional views of what it means to be a Latina expected to restrict herself to a woman's place in her family and her community. These pressures produce high turnover rates as women activists succumb to pressures at home. As Monreal Molina of OPI put it, "After all, we are basically a very vulnerable group, I'd say an at-risk group — to be a woman is difficult." Monreal Molina pointed to all the factors that conspire against women as marginal citizens of their societies. She also noted that the financial situation of many border families creates a host of other pressures. Often, women bear the burden of a family's breakup, becoming sole heads of households. Ironically, as organizations like Mujeres Unidas and OPI help women financially empower themselves and their families, that very independence has led to family breakups, which in turn have become increasingly important for women's NGOs to address.

Monreal Molina noted that "in effect women['s becoming] wage earners and . . . community activists leads to having men feel inadequate in their households given the culture where these men and women have been socialized to see men as primary breadwinners."

Men have lost their traditional roles, and this has generated a serious crisis, including, in my opinion, . . . a lot of violence against women, because men have pent up resentment toward women when they have not been able to find jobs. They think to themselves, "I no longer rule at home," leaving them with the feeling that they no longer have a relevant role to play in the family. And that many men do not forgive.

Consequently, "the challenges that women face in the border region are many" (Staudt and Coronado 2002: 156). Along with a patriarchal society that marginalizes women are maquiladoras and immigration politics that conspire to pit workers against each other. That is why collaborating with other women's groups across cities like El Paso and Ciudad Juárez has become critical to women's NGO success on both sides of the border.

Women's border struggles face the same issues on both sides of the Rio Grande. Women's issues are human rights issues, and this has led the NGOs to confront maquiladoras, city government, violence against women, homelessness, sickness, and other threats to border women. Opportunities for border women to organize remain focused on local strategies embedded in local networks, which is why, unlike in Michoacán, in Ciudad Juárez and El Paso, the Beijing conference came and went with little fanfare. The Beijing preparatory events did provide a moment, however, in the form of a Chihuahua state meeting, where women's NGOs from El Paso and Ciudad Juárez came together to articulate what women's struggles and feminism meant for them.

THE IMPACT OF THE BEIJING CONFERENCE ON WOMEN
IN EL PASO / CIUDAD JUÁREZ

Two women representing La Mujer Obrera went to Beijing. But many who did not go to Beijing participated in the Chihuahua "Toward Beijing" preparatory process. This began long before the conference. As representatives of Centro Mujeres de Fe y Esperanza, Lorenza Zuniga, a board member, and Ida Berresheim attended a 1994 La Raza program in Boulder, Colorado, as well as another meeting in Gallup to contribute to the Beijing conference agenda. "These meetings really showed the diversity of women that the preparations for Beijing engaged," Berresheim said. "Much of the preparations included workshops that brought together not only Latinas and Native American women but others, including university women, and women from religious congregations that created opportunities for ethnic and other diversity. Six women from our congregation went and [as did ones from] other sister centers [in] the United States and Canada." Despite these efforts, participation among border women's NGOs was limited.

Monreal Molina of OPI said that a main reason why many Ciudad Juárez women's groups did not participate was that "the coordination [for Beijing] was in Chihuahua [the capital of the state of Chihuahua, quite a distance from Ciudad Juárez]. And, somehow Juárez has been disconnected from Chihuahua. . . . Consequently, those who mostly participated were women from Chihuahua, and, well, we understood that they represented all of us." OPI and other women's NGOs from Ciudad Juárez and El Paso did participate in the Segundo Encuentro Estatal de Mujeres de Chihuahua (Second State Meeting of Women of Chihuahua). The gathering took place March 5–7, 1999 in Ciudad Juárez. Some 240 women attended the three-day event, and as many as sixty-seven women's NGOs were represented, from fourteen different border communities, including Ciudad Juárez and El Paso, though most of the NGOs present were from Mexico City (Report: Secondo Encuentro Estatal de Mujeres de Chihuahua or Second State Encounter of the Women of Chihuahua, 1999). Among the seven NGOs that organized the event, three were women's faith-based organizations.

Gringas Aguirre of the Centro Mujeres Tonantzín noted that her center was barely two years old when the preparations for Beijing began. She highlighted the connection at the conference to women's faith-based NGOs. In fact, the Centro Mujeres Tonantzín, which helped to organize the Segundo Encuentro Estatal de Mujeres de Chihuahua in collaboration with other women's NGOs, was joined by other women's faith-based NGOs including Mujeres para el Diálogo (Women for Dialogue, or MPD, based in Mexico City). MPD's collaboration with women's NGOs of Chihuahua is important to mention for two reasons. First, it underscores the connection between border women and other women's communities. Dolores Navarrete, representing the Ciudad Juárez side of the Centro Mujeres de Fe y

Esperanza (also known in Ciudad Juárez as Centro Santa Catarina), in her welcoming address to the women gathered for the Segundo Encuentro Estatal noted that "at first I was going to say that we should be proud to be Mexican women, but in analyzing the word [*woman*] more profoundly I realize that the word *woman* has no nationality, because everything is based on being a woman" (Segundo Encuentro Estatal de Mujeres de Chihuahua document 1999: 2–3). Second, the conference participants' choice of themes important to border women underscores the global emphasis on women's issues. These themes included health, sexuality, labor and migration, intrafamily violence, public security, and pastoral work.

In all, the Segundo Encuentro Estatal provided, in the words of Francesca Montoya, who commented on the overall Beijing process, "an opportunity for border women to make some of the broader connections necessary to sustain women's organizing." More important, the Segundo Encuentro Estatal ended with proposals to broaden networking and exchange with other women's NGOs. The women offered several strategies, including sharing newsletters, creating calendars announcing events, writing to the governor of Chihuahua and the state's representative to the Mexican House of Congress asking them to confront the murders of women in the Juárez desert, and publishing a directory of local women's NGOs.

Donna Kustusch of Mujeres de Fe y Esperanza in Ciudad Juárez underscored how important the state meeting was for area women. As she noted:

I think for the women in Juárez there is now the sense that we are connected to a broader global women's movement, which gives us the hope and the spirit and the determination that we need to keep going. . . . Women see that because people come into their lives from the United States and elsewhere, you know there is a broader movement and that gives them the kind of courage that they need to keep going and keep asking the questions and to know that they are connected to something bigger than themselves.

Montoya also noted that one of greatest achievements of the Beijing process was bringing so many representatives of grassroots women's efforts to an international stage. For Montoya, who did go to Beijing, it was something "to be at a conference where you had the opportunity to meet women from other countries, where you have an opportunity to not only share what you're doing, the work that you're doing, and who you are, but what you're about and what you're hoping to accomplish, what you're working toward." It was, Montoya added, enough "to share that and get feedback, but at the same time listen to what other women are doing, it's such a unique opportunity to come back . . . energized about who you are and what you're doing, and not to think that 'oh, I must be crazy because I'm the only one doing this'; it's an opportunity for you to be around other women and get ideas."

Such testimonies show that international exchanges provide opportunities not only for sharing ideas, but to regain energy. As Montoya put it, "You come back refreshed, you come back with a bigger vision. . . . you make the connection between what you're doing here and what's happening elsewhere, and the networks, the possibility for networking are endless . . . endless."

Women attending the Segundo Encuentro Estatal de Mujeres de Chihuahua called for more meetings to take place and extended a special invitation to Sister Leonor Aída of MPD and others linked to faith-based women's organizations to attend the upcoming Encuentro Nacional de Mujeres Cristianas (National Meeting of Christian Women). This religious connection and the experiences Latinas have with women's faith-based NGOs are typical of alliances Latinas are forging as they blaze their path in women's movements. These alliances with religious groups are part of the larger Latina/o story.

"The increase in women's participation is pretty evident," Monreal Molina said, "and above all if we take into account historically how Mexican women's roles have been typified to look like something else. But I do believe that the advances have . . . had an impact. Above all, women in the United States and Latinas are involved in planning, each from her place and from her own historical reference." In the next chapter we will explore the historical factors leading to the emergence of women's faith-based NGOs. What is key is that forming alliances and coalitions with like-minded women's groups allows women's communities to achieve goals that otherwise would be out of reach.

On this point Montoya remarked, "I think one of the unique things when

I worked in our organization was how we were involved locally, in doing the local organizing. At the same time, those who are founders of organizations understood that you could not just operate locally. Your focus, your vision, has to be far greater than that." Women's faith-based NGOs share in that vision, enabling them to make crucial contributions to Latina activism.

CHAPTER THREE

The Religious Connection

In 1972, the women's sector of the Confederación Latinoamericana de Religiosos (Confederation of Latin American Religious, or CLAR) lobbied for their organization to include women's issues in its platform. The women members encouraged each other to find their identity and mission as women committed to working in their churches (CLAR 1972). The Catholic nun Eleonor Aida Concha, a cofounder of Mujeres para el Diálogo (Women for Dialogue, or MPD) explained that the initial reflective process evolved into activism among Catholic sisters in Mexico.

> When I decided to participate [in the women's movement] there was no Christian women's movement per se consolidated in Mexico. What there was were Christian women who shared feelings of uneasiness. We started meeting from time to time with specific invitations from Betsy Hollands [founder of Comunicación Intercambio y Desarrollo Humano en América Latina (Communication, Exchange, and Human Development in Latin America, or CIDHAL), an NGO based in Cuernavaca]. Several sisters from my congregation had been collaborating with her in a systematic way — that is, more institutionally. I collaborated with them [CIDHAL] on specific issues. About four sisters, that I remember, from my congregation were involved in those early years, collaborating with the organization founded by Betsy Hollands. I later worked with the Indigenous Commission of Bishops, where I struck a chord

with the women question. I have often said that in the heart of every woman there is a feminist, because it became obvious to me that in your own suffering, a series of questions emerge, above all within the [Catholic] church. It is then that you begin to gain consciousness that this should not be—that you are marginalized and repressed. Later you hear talk that there are women trying to do something, at least initially at a level of reflection.

By 1979, reflection turned into action with international meetings on the status of women in the Latin American Catholic Church.

In Mexico, one of the more publicized events took place in Puebla on the occasion of the Third Conferencia Episcopal Latinoamericana (Latin American Bishops' Conference, or CELAM). MPD, which had been founded earlier that year, coordinated a gathering to protest the status of women where participants presented papers and discussed liberation theology. The papers revealed the emphasis that Latin American women placed on economic and political oppression in their analysis of capitalism and the inherited system of colonial patriarchy. In a press release, the participants declared that they had gathered to examine the role of women in church institutions and to criticize liberation theology for not addressing women's oppression. As Concha related, MPD crystallized in 1979 because the CELAM meeting forced women there to articulate and debate what such a group should be about. In 1980, the women who formed MPD published a statement of the organization's specific goals and mission.

According to Concha, in the beginning the women saw MPD as an organization "to disseminate information." But they also saw it as part of "a women's movement that engaged the Catholic Church, pushing for women in ministry, specifically the priesthood, and the possibility of doing theology from a new [feminist] perspective." Early on, the issues were more about creating space for participation in a Christian women's movement. "We gave the [Christian feminist] women's movement a political character which did not exist at the time." For the women of MPD, feminist issues had to be elevated to feminist activism. Prior to 1979, Concha said, those who wanted the Catholic Church to make its relationship with women more equitable were only talking and writing among themselves.

I remember a document put forth by the women religious of CLAR [1972]. . . . Thus, at first, there were attempts to work with . . . CLAR, but I never accepted, . . . possibly because, like many Mexican women, I was too entrenched in a cultural value that was very nationalistic, and so what we wanted to do we wanted to do in Mexico. We didn't want to do it at the Latin American level [which was the focus of CLAR]. Now, some of my sisters have gone in that direction, to the [broader] Latin American level, myself included, because we turned to study the issues at broader levels . . . so I and we could do better work. But early on my focus was in relation to work I was doing in the women's movement [in Mexico]. In the 1960s, there was the challenging work of Betsy Hollands. Great strides were made from the 1960s to 1979. . . . These were the precursors [of MPD].

Hollands's call to confront the Catholic bishops pulled Concha and others into the women's movement. The 1979 meeting in Puebla not only launched MPD, it brought together women from all over Latin America, North America, and Europe. "I felt this was a real important moment, because it allowed us, at the church level, to debate [our issues] even if the bishops laughed at us." In Puebla, MPD formulated positions on women, religion, their churches, and the impact of patriarchal dominance supported by religious institutions and their ideologies. More important, Concha noted, the meeting showed the women that despite their different origins, they could communicate across borders, as well as across differences of culture and class.

From that very moment [the 1979 Puebla MPD meeting] you could see the differences in our ideas of what we thought feminism should be. The North Americans put emphasis on the priesthood. The Latin Americans put emphasis on women from the popular sector. We came together [in our agreement] that doing theology without taking on the [religious] institution that neither understood nor accepted us made no sense. And because liberation theology was in its heyday, that gave us enough of a foundation to think that we could work from the base and from there do [feminist] theology. So the first thing that happened [at the Puebla meeting] . . . was developing a gender consciousness.

Buttressing Concha's memory of MPD's origins is the group's 1979 press statement describing itself as an international women's organization, comprised primarily of Latin American women, that began with a small group of Mexicans gathered in Puebla on the occasion of the Third Latin American Bishops' Conference. The statement also declared that "the objective of Mujeres para el Diálogo in Puebla is to establish dialogue between ourselves and bishops, theologians, and others present as friends." The purpose of the conference was to bring into focus women's position in the Catholic Church. "Women have been marginalized from church participation, and the most oppressed women in the church are women religious, who have made significant contributions to the church, but who have largely gone unrecognized for their work and have not had control over their lives or activities." This reality for women in the Catholic Church was linked to larger problems facing Latin American women.

At the meeting, Carmen Lora presented a paper, "La teología de la liberación y la mujer" ("Liberation Theology and Women"), that underscored two critical aspects of women's oppression in Latin America. She argued that women's oppression in this region generally has two faces: that of patriarchal power and that of Latin America's historic and economic status since European colonization. Both, she said, are rooted, first, in the establishment of a male-centered religion, Catholicism, and, second, in the passing from colonial to capitalist exploitation, as economic power shifted from mercantilist Spain and Portugal to countries, such as the United States and the Soviet Union, that dominated the postcolonial world. These factors cannot be ignored, because as Lora asserts most Latin American women come from the popular classes, which is why liberation theology was so well received there.

Liberation theology facilitated the understanding of religion's concrete historical role in society. It critiqued religious and other social institutions as products of an economic system mired first in colonization and then in capitalism. Christian feminists like those in MPD analyzed Latin American history to push for a theology that expressed religio-cultural aspects of the human condition. In other words, they advocated a religion and theology that did not separate itself from an analysis of the inherited colonial institutions that link it to Latin America's present socioeconomic reality. Several papers presented at the conference underscored the importance of this type of analysis. While concerned primarily with the status of women in religious institutions, the women gathered at Puebla argued that the oppression of women was a manifestation of larger economic, political, and ideological problems. Presenters tended to synthesize discussions of the role of women in the church with ones of women's roles in the family, as workers, in class struggles, and in political organizations. They also expressed concern about the status of indigenous women. Roxanna Carrillo (1990:201), cofounder of Centro de la Mujer Peruana Flora Tristan (Flora Tristan Center for Peruvian Women), has reflected on why indigenous women became central to the movement.

> Living in a small country with very limited resources teaches you that surviving politically requires adding up your efforts in order not to disappear. Peru is also a country in which a large majority of women live in poverty, most of them of Andean descent, which makes us aware that if we are to work for the development of a strong women's movement, we must cross the class and race barriers that divide our country. Thus much of the organizing carried out by feminist groups in Peru in the last decade has happened in the slums or shantytowns that surround the major cities, which is true for most of the countries in the region. There is an interesting and potentially powerful political chemistry, which is creating new political consciousness and alliances among women.

It is precisely the recognition of this new political consciousness that led me to focus in this book on the voices of religious feminist and nonreligious women's organizations.

The Latin American Christian feminists at the 1979 conference discussed a number of other broader concerns important to the women's movement, petitioning the Catholic Church to:

> revise its ideas about nature and the function of women, which reduce women to roles in the home;
> foster the communitarian care of children so women can be free to participate fully in the global social sphere;
> support women's rights to control their own bodies;

recognize women's rights to participate in shaping the direction of the church at all levels;

call for reflection on women as objects and subjects of theology; and support, theologically and in pastoral work, solidarity with women struggling for the liberation of their people.

This last demand shows that women in faith-based organizations are cognizant of broader women's issues and their groups' connections to other movements. Final remarks at the Puebla meeting called for solidarity with all women in Latin America, particularly those then living under dictatorships in Nicaragua, Chile, Argentina, Brazil, and Guatemala. Speakers noted that these women were persecuted, tortured, and lost loved ones as a result of their commitment to fight for the liberation of their people — a commitment that the women at the conference proclaimed they shared. As we will see, similar themes surfaced at other meetings.

THE LATIN AMERICAN AND CARIBBEAN FEMINIST CONFERENCE (1983)

Two years after the Puebla encounter, approximately three hundred women met in Bogotá to call for talks with Latin American governments on dismantling patriarchal power. Another two years after that, the Second Latin American and Caribbean Feminist Conference, held in Lima, focused on patriarchy. According to a June 1984 Isis International report ("Reporte del Encuentro Feminista Latino Americano y del Caribe"), six hundred women gathered in Lima for workshops including "Patriarchy and the Church." The Maryknoll sister Rosa Dominga Trapasso presented a paper titled "Iglesia, mujer y feminismo" ("Church, Women, and Feminism"). Trapasso is an important figure because, like Concha of MPD, she bridges the world of feminist Christians and that of the larger women's movement.

Trapasso had been an activist in the women's movement for many years and was one of ninety-seven signers to a statement on pluralism and free choice in abortion published October 7, 1984, in the *New York Times*. She and other signers came to international attention when Pope John Paul II threatened to expel them from their congregations if they did not retract the statement. In many respects, the Vatican's threat accomplished its goal, because some women were forced to resign from their congregations and others lost their jobs. But the tactic also backfired because many congregations did not force women who signed the document to renounce it. In their book *No Turning Back* (1990), two signers of the *New York Times* statement, Barbara Ferraro and Patricia Hussey, denounced the Vatican's attempt to restrict what they considered a basic freedom to dissent publicly from official church policies. They noted that the Vatican's stance showed the extent to which women were subject to the church's patriarchal authority. The book's publication underscored the frustration many women felt at their powerlessness in dealing with Catholic religious authorities. Some of the congregations, to satisfy the Vatican, worked on statements of "clarification" rather than "retraction." Many of the congregations did so while trying to maintain the integrity of the signers' position on abortion rights. But Mary Hunt and Frances Kissling (1987) were critical of how the clarifications were handled. They reported that some of the signers did not participate in the writing of the clarifications. In other instances, congregations put unrelenting pressure on the signers to come to quick solutions satisfactory to the Vatican.

Despite the setbacks that came with the incident surrounding the *New York Times* ad, the mood in both the United States and Latin America was one of defiance against Vatican authority, especially because the Vatican epitomized the concentration of male power. At the last plenary session of the Second Latin American and Caribbean Feminist Conference, several documents were presented that urged greater defiance of patriarchal authority, particularly as promulgated by the Catholic Church. According to the 1984 Isis International workshop report, several documents contained proposals that called for expanding the Latin American and Caribbean feminist movement. But some women felt strongly that neither the first conference nor the second had taken real action to further the examination of women's oppression by the Catholic Church. The authors of the proposals declared that "to be a feminist in Latin America and the Caribbean means to analyze society as capitalist and patriarchal" (quoted in "Reporte del Encuentro Feminista Latino Americano y del Caribe"). They also argued that the feminist movement, as a social and political movement, should clearly state its goal to be the elimination of imperialism, capitalism, and patriarchy. For them there was no socialism without the liberation of women and no liberation of women without socialism. The same themes surfaced at other gatherings on women, religion, and theology, including, most notably, those sponsored by the Ecumenical Association of Third World Theologians (EATWOT).

In 1985, two years after the Latin American and Caribbean women's conference in Lima, twenty-eight women from nine Latin American countries gathered in Buenos Aires for the conference "Theology from the Perspective of Women" (Tamez 1989: 150–53). The participants noted:

> In our celebration in Buenos Aires, we asked questions about methods and what mediations we used in our theological activity. We were surprised to note that the characteristics that we discovered amount to our own method and that these mediations embrace a whole range of possibilities that can take expression in many languages. Social sciences, psychology, linguistics, philosophy, sociology of religion, ecology, and other sciences are present there and are woven with the Bible, Tradition, and Life — our unifying and inclusive way of perceiving life. (ibid.: 152)

The focus on universal understandings of oppression resonated with women in more broadly defined feminist circles. By 1990, discussion and debate on the role of women in church institutions was important enough that support for workshops at larger feminist conferences continued. One of these encounters took place again in San Bernardo, Argentina in 1990, organized as part of the Fifth Latin American and Caribbean Feminist Conference.

WOMEN IN RELIGION AT THE FIFTH
FEMINIST CONFERENCE (1990)

In a report compiled by Trapasso and available at Talitha Cumi, a feminist Christian organization cofounded by Trapaso in Lima, the solid ties of feminist Christians to larger feminist organizations are more than evident. The networking across organizations manifests in women's support for each other's groups. Trapasso herself is on the advisory board of the magazine *Viva*, published by the Lima-based feminist organization Flora Tristan. She also is active in nonreligious affiliated feminist organizations inside and outside Peru, including Isis International, which has an office in Santiago, Chile. The international character of the Latin American women's movement also is evident in the number of conferences that attract women from throughout the region.

Trapasso reported that at the Fifth Latin American and Caribbean Feminist Conference, the workshop on women and religion attracted women from countries including Argentina, Brazil, Venezuela, Mexico, Chile, Uruguay, Peru, Bolivia, Nicaragua, and El Salvador. Non–Latin American women who attended the conference and workshop represented Holland, Spain, the United States, Ireland, and Germany. For the most part, the women who took part in the religion workshop described themselves as primarily active in Catholic and Protestant churches, but others reported no religious institutional affiliation. In fact, the list of participants shows that most belonged to feminist organizations whose main function was not necessarily religious.

Of the fifty-six participants who attended the workshop on women and religion, thirteen gave mailing addresses of women's organizations with no specific religious affiliation, and seven gave addresses of women's organizations with both a feminist and a religious focus. The other participants gave home addresses or post office boxes, and for a few NGO affiliation could not be determined. But like the women of CLAR and MPD, the participants in the 1990 workshop on women in religion expressed concern over the impact of male-centered religions on their lives, as Trapasso's report notes. It was one reason why the women gathered in Argentina pushed for a spirituality that was distinctly feminist: "Without ceasing to be a church and without creating parallelisms, it is our desire to be able to create communities where we can express our faith in a democratic and plural church that is oriented toward a future whose vision is rooted in equality and liberty" (reflection group report, quoted in Trapasso 1990: 1). In strategizing on how to meet these goals, the workshop participants divided themselves into groups reflecting on four areas: new expressions of spirituality, sexuality, the fifth centennial celebration of Columbus's voyage, and transforming the structures of churches. More than half the women opted to participate in the "new expressions of spirituality" reflection group.

The workshop was successful not only for the advances made in the discussions, but because the women left the workshop committed to maintaining lines of communication with others who had attended. They committed themselves to developing a network of feminist groups in search of a feminist spirituality and theology. The women exchanged names and addresses, a list that would be circulated to produce a network of women interested in continuing debate and articulating their concerns publicly. Similar forums were made possible by women's participation in other venues, including the Grupo Ecuménico de Mujeres (Ecumenical Women's Group) of Uruguay; the Encuentro Latinoamericano de Mujeres y Hombres en la Iglesia (Latin American Gathering of Women and Men in the Church), held in San José, Costa Rica, in 1981; the Comisión de Mujeres (Women's Commission–Ecumenical Association of Third World Theologians, EATWOT, or ASETT: Asociación Ecuménica de Teólogas y Teólogos del Tercer Mundo), which organized the Conferencia Intercontinental de Teólogas del Tercer Mundo in Oaxtepec, Mexico, in 1986; the Departamento Ecuménico de Investigación (Ecumenical Research Department) in San José, Costa Rica; and Equipo de Mujeres en Acción Solidaria (Team of Women United in Acción, or EMAS) in Morelia, Michoacán; among others.

EMAS AND THE CHALLENGE TO THE CHURCH

EMAS's connection to faith-based perspectives is embodied by one of its cofounders, Maruja González Butrón. As I noted in chapter 2, before González Butrón went to EMAS her social activism had been rooted in progressive Catholic teachings, beginning with her student years at the Universidad Católica in Lima, in Catholic Action organizations. The social teachings of Catholic Action were nurtured further by her ties and friendship with the liberation theologian Father Gustavo Gutierrez, her marriage to Raúl Vidales, one of Mexico's foremost liberation theologians, and her early affiliation with MPD after she moved to Mexico. That early connection to MPD and her work with CIDHAL turned her attention to a social activism focused on women. Her feminist awakening began as she and others around her questioned church institutions and women's positions in them, given the patriarchal structure and teachings of religious institutions. But as González

Butrón told me in our interview, it was at a 1978 ecumenical church event in Mexico City that her feminist consciousness really awakened. "Living here in Mexico in 1978 there was an ecumenical event that marked my life very much. I discovered that there were many women like me who were active in their own churches . . . that had or shared concerns about the future of their churches, because they considered them very patriarchal. They were very discriminatory toward women and there was barely talk of women's issues; they focused rather on families."

The women at the Mexico City meeting noted that the church structures were fundamentally masculine, with leadership positions reserved for men. For González Butrón and the women at that 1978 meeting and other meetings she attended subsequently, including those sponsored by EATWOT, their questions about women's marginalization within church institutions could no longer be contained. "It was wonderful to discover that there were women . . . who were working in the field of theology, from the perspective of women, what is now called feminist theology," said González Butrón. Other women there, many from Catholic circles like her, were "working out of the social sciences in popular movements as theologians, doing theology. . . . the Brazilian women in particular impressed me so much because they brought so many issues they were working on to the field of feminist theology." But those who influenced González Butrón most at the time were women in the social sciences as well as theologians both inside and outside of Mexico. An economist, González Butrón was most influenced early by "Teresa Cavalcanti; Carmen Lora of Peru, though [she is] not a theologian; María Pilar Aquino; Elsa Tamez; . . . Yvonne Guevara; . . . and Nancy Cardoso of Brazil," among others. A number of these women presented papers at the 1979 MPD meeting in Puebla. We will examine some of the topics and issues they focused on later in this chapter.

But other faith-based women's organizations and their leaders came to influence González Butrón, among them Católicas por el Derecho a Decidir (Catholic Women for the Right to Choose) and Talitha Cumi through the work of Rosa Dominga Trapasso. González Butrón described Trapasso as "a woman religious, a Catholic sister with vows [una mujer consagrada] who identifies with women's issues and women from the popular sector in particular, and who challenges ecclesial structures." For González Butrón, women share in the same marginalization whether they are laity like herself or nuns like Trapasso. Despite resistance from and battles with church institutions, González Butrón and others continue to champion women's causes, but from within their churches. Church communities are spaces where many women turn for spiritual comfort and empowerment. As González Butrón put it, "I continue in this church because I believe there are seeds for change that have been planted. . . . I believe we can continue to plant seeds. I believe there are many women who think the same way, some fear expressing their views, but others work from within to produce change, a more effective strategy than if we worked from outside."

González Butrón has translated her brand of feminism into an activism that engages faith-based groups, primarily by connecting it to faith-based activism focused on community struggles. Much of her vision comes out of experiences that she and others had working with the base Christian community model often associated with liberation theology. But talking about base Christian communities is taboo in Michoacán, because the church hierarchy follows a conservative Catholic line and condemns liberation theology. Conservatives see base Christian communities and the type of community work they engage in as political activism inappropriate for churches. But women like González Butrón find other ways to do the grassroots work that for them is grounded in a faith inspired by liberation theology and Catholic Action. This has led González Butrón to work with the poorest communities in Michoacán: its indigenous villages. "A church that is committed," she said, "a church of the poor, can be created in a number of venues outside ecclesial spaces. I believe very deeply that the work we do in communities supporting indigenous women is one way of doing and living the church — that is, constructing the church. I don't see it any other way." González Butrón's community work and her feminist activism thus reflect the bridging of her experiences in liberationist and feminist circles. Her faith and feminist vision, she said, are "a struggle for justice, for the defense of human rights, and for those most dispossessed in society." Consequently, feminists who have come from the teachings of Catholic Action and liberation theology believe that the Catholic Church's "preferential option" for the poor (a term associated with the 1979 CELAM meeting and one that reveals the influence of liberation theology) indicates that its hierarchy can be transformed. But despite the support of liberation theology by progressive bishops, women like González Butrón are frustrated with the institutional entrenchment of a Catholic hierarchy that resists allowing women to lead in the church.

For many feminists working for change in their churches, liberation theology has proven to be of little consequence, because few liberation theologians specifically address women's marginalization in society, much less in churches. In a 1988 interview Trapasso noted that over the centuries "the [Catholic] Church has seen itself as power, control, paternalistic, and the poor as dependent on [it] as dutiful sons and daughters" (Peña 1995b). The same accusations were repeated in interviews with other feminist activists whose community projects were complicated by organizational disagreements with local progressive bishops or priests. More often they are opposed by local clergy when they seek to fund women's programs or take public stands on abortion (Peña 1995a). For many women working within their churches, whether the hierarchy is conservative or progressive makes little difference: it remains a male-dominated structure.

González Butrón does not want to abandon her church just because it is patriarchal and resists feminists like her. But she noted that during its early history, the women's movement in Mexico had little contact with religious groups and women's groups in base Christian communities.

I'm referring to a period that I actually experienced very little of myself, because it was before I came to the movement. But there was a great distance between the [feminist] movement and . . . the Christian women from base Christian communities. Despite that, I've observed since the early 1980s a great effort to reach out on the part of feminist Christian women. In the process they [Catholic women's groups] became feminist organizations as in the case of Mujeres para el Diálogo, a group that . . . became feminist in the 1980s without denying its Christian identity. This was very important. . . . There is in the Mexican church a sector of progressive women already ahead on women's issues and that works on these issues. There are also on the other side very conservative women in the pro-life movement defending a very conservative position within the [Catholic] Church. These are the ones who can count on the church hierarchy's support. I don't want to be a pessimist, but I feel that all the proposals that we've made in the last year [in preparation for Beijing], as Christian women, as part of a larger women's movement in Mexico, to take to Beijing were not supported or well received by the church hierarchy.

González Butrón's frustration arises from the little success that feminists like her have had in changing the institutional workings of their religious institutions. But she takes comfort in the ability of feminist theologians to produce challenging feminist critiques in their writings. She sees this as an important step in challenging the ideological foundations of patriarchal power in religious institutions. She is heartened by feminist activism in community work, which has undermined church hierarchies even when women are threatened with censure.

Despite these threats, women continue their faith-based community work, challenging their communities to think critically not only about issues that affect them as poor communities, but also about how poor women are twice marginalized. Indigenous communities add a third dimension, racism, to the women's critique. In these contexts, women's strategies include producing materials to ground discussion in workshops, allowing them to focus on human rights as a women's concern. Among the issues González Butrón noted were women's "rights over their bodies, sexuality, something that hardly anyone talked about before, and now they've even produced projects where they incorporate these themes into their formation workshops." Even limited success has been reason for her to take comfort. "Many grassroots women . . . are feminists . . . and there are religious women who identify themselves as feminists, and others who even though they don't identify themselves as such at least assume less submissive roles and have creatively made spaces for themselves in their churches."

Another opening for faith-based women has been the creation of ecumenical groups like the Asociación de Pastoras (Association of Women Pastors), based in Mexico City. One of this group's key figures is Alma Tamez, sister of Elsa Tamez, the famed feminist biblical scholar that González Butrón mentioned as key to shaping her theological feminist perspective. The connection to Alma and to Elsa Tamez underscores the ecumenical dimension of women's faith-based communities, since the Tamez sisters are Protestant. For all these women, confronting patriarchal dominance is the key, regardless of their faith tradition. In her interview with me, Alma Tamez described how she developed her Christian feminist perspective. For Tamez feminism means challenging male-centered biblical interpretations by noting that in the original biblical Hebrew texts often no male-centered meaning was intended. She challenges male colleagues by saying, "'My brother, but it says here [in the Bible] that women and men were both made in the same image of God, both of them.' They come back at me with, 'But it [the Bible] says that women are subjects of their husbands as they are to God,' to which I say this is a strategy on men's part to oppress us; and this was how I grew, vis-à-vis the Bible, [reading it] from women's perspectives." By targeting biblical interpretations, "one learns and grows," and these rereadings feed a developing Christian feminism. Tamez finds that she is able to confront the patriarchal ideologies embedded in biblical interpretations more effectively because of support from networks that include women like González Butrón.

Other networks for Tamez included the Unión Nacional de Sociedades Femeninas (National Union of Women's Societies), which has more than six hundred women members and where Tamez is most active, as well as the Mujeres de la Conferencia Cristiana por la Paz (Women of the Christian Conference for Peace), "which challenges women to focus also on race and class issues," she said. International participation in women's organizations also was critical for her. She mentioned in particular the Conferencia Latinoamericana de Iglesias (Latin American Council of Churches, or CLAI) and the Red de Teólogas de Costa Rica (Network of Women Theologians of Costa Rica). According to Tamez, these organizations are important most notably for identifying strategies "that confront patriarchy's hold on religious institutions." Building the ideal church, Tamez noted, would require

reading the Bible, but from the perspective of women. It is one way to remove the wall [that has kept women out]. I've been dissatisfied, we need new tools, hermeneutical tools, biblical experts, with new analyses, people with knowledge to look for new working tools because we are stuck. . . . they tell you that you are a subversive, that you are this or that, but here I am holding national positions. I did not want them, but my husband advised me that if I wanted to make changes that I needed to be inside [the institutions]. It is not a question of power, but of service. So here I am representing the National Union on the Commission of Education. [This is a separate entity from the school, which is called the Escuela Bíblica Central (Central Bible School)].

Tamez also thought she could be of service to the movement by "continuing to raise women's consciousness; that is the permanent struggle, to show them our reality and elevate their self-esteem more than anything. This is permanent and constant." And though Tamez finds that the women's movement has had limited success transforming women's roles in the Mexican church, she remains hopeful: "One should not lose patience. . . . we cannot force others to think how we think, but it is imperative to propose new methods. As women, we need to look for new strategies, and here we need real help."

Some new strategies were in evidence in the way Tamez and González Butrón came to work together in nonfeminist circles, including in the Conferencia Cristiana por la Paz (Christian Conference for Peace, or CCP). "CCP was founded around 1984," Tamez recalled. "I got involved in Nicaragua, where we had a nice gathering with Comandante Borges [Tomás Borges, minister of the interior in the Sandinista government]. He had invited us and joined us for a meeting. After that I became more involved. And by 1985 I already had several responsibilities that I came to share with Maru [González Butrón]." Here Alma Tamez points to their need to be part of several circles when building feminist faith communities. In doing so, women like Tamez and González Butrón look to create venues where women and men can be equal. "We have to create participatory democracy and develop theologies that support this vision," González Butrón said. This is also central to developing new models for community work, moving from male hierarchal relations to feminist inclusive paradigms. While liberation theology importantly highlighted class oppression that affects both men and women, it has been criticized for ignoring women's status. The first step in overcoming this limitation is for men and women to do community work together. González Butrón asked, "What use is [liberation theology] — though I recognize that Leonardo [Boff] and other theologians are open [to this critique]" — if women continue to be marginalized in our societies? For feminist critics of religious institutions and the theology that upholds them, changing social structures requires producing theology that constructs new paradigms for men and women to work together. But, González Butrón said, producing such feminist discourse in the world of theology is a daunting struggle.

> There are feminist theologians, but there also are feminist theories that are not Christian or they are post-Christian that women really have not had a chance to respond to, and I say let's go to it. So I have formed a group to discuss our concerns. It is called the Círculo de Reflección Teológica Feminista Sor Juana Inés de la Cruz [Sor Juan Inés de la Cruz Feminist Theological Reflection Circle], precisely because I see us at a moment where we are too dispersed. . . . I think it is time. I have wanted to do this for a long time, since my days in Mujeres para el Diálogo, to create a moment for us to publish in theology. . . . We now have people, not many, but enough to form reflection groups on systematic theology.

These groups have come a long way in their readiness to produce both challenging feminist theologies and models for doing community work.

"My role now is to help realize wherever possible a challenge by women with a more global focus," said González Butrón, voicing a common sentiment. In other words, she seeks to address gender issues with other women's communities across geographic and ethnic borders. This is why the 1995 Beijing conference was so important. "Anyone who bumps up against society questions its culture," she said. "It is a patriarchal, authoritarian, and machista culture we share globally and economically. . . . We have to develop strategies [to support one another], you by doing one thing, we by doing others. I feel women have been at the forefront of this wonderful revolution that is taking place." González Butrón noted that "all the noise" we women organizers have created has indeed made a difference, particularly in the lives of the women who are engaged in the process of producing major social change. The success of faith-based community work lies in the transformation and empowerment of women involved in it. As we have already seen, community activism provides the context for women to develop gender consciousness.

BORDER WOMEN'S FAITH-BASED COALITIONS IN EL PASO/CIUDAD JUAREZ

In Ciudad Juárez and El Paso, the social forces that impacted feminists in Mexico and elsewhere in Latin America also shaped their thinking and mobilization. The opening up of the Catholic Church to progressive thinking beginning with the Second Vatican Council of the early 1960s was taken up at bishops' conferences in Latin America and the United States. Pope John XXIII began a series of sweeping changes in church policy that were picked up by Pope Paul VI after John XXIII's death. With these popes came a new liberalism in the Catholic Church that facilitated exchange between Christians and Marxists focusing on first world nations and their exploitation of third world people. This theme, central in liberation theology, also has shaped discussions in U.S. feminist circles, particularly among feminists of color. The economic focus of this discussion is important, because, as women of color and global feminists charge, continuing dependent development and the globalization of capitalism are at the heart of global poverty and the way it touches women, and disproportionately women of color.

By focusing on capitalism liberation theologians contributed to this discussion, insisting that transforming society meant transforming a way of life that privileged some and marginalized others. In the words of Gutiérrez (1973: 273), "Everywhere people were coming to the realization that the class struggle had become part of Latin America's economic, social, political, cultural, and religious reality." This recognition extended beyond Latin America to shape the attitudes of progressives, many of whom ended up in community work, whether in the *colonias*, the barrios, or the base Christian communities of Mexico and U.S.-Mexico border cities. The lives of most of the people doing community work in Michoacán and El Paso/Ciudad Juárez were touched by Vatican II, liberation theology, feminist theory (including theology), and other events and movements that promoted progressive thinking in Catholic and Protestant circles.

For example, Rubén García underscored the influence of these events on workers at El Paso's Annunciation House when he described their living a spirituality committed to the border's poor. "Annunciation House was about looking inwardly and saying how can we live our lives with greater meaning, with more purpose. . . . We approached it from a faith-based perspective as we went through that year [1978, when Annunciation House was founded]; and as we reflected on scripture, we could not get away from the realization of the special relationship that exists between God and oppressed people, God and those who are poor, God and those who are marginalized, excluded, etc." Similarly, Patricia Monreal Molina of the Organización Popular Independiente (OPI) in Ciudad Juárez, another NGO in this network, noted that the people who created OPI came to community work from parish activities. Several of OPI's founders started organizing in the base Christian communities on the edge of Ciudad Juárez.

While base Christian communities emerged in many Catholic areas, initially as a response to priest shortages in Latin America, they are known today for allowing lay leaders to assume broader roles than traditional Catholic parishes permit and for advancing decentralized and participatory community leadership. They thus bear little resemblance to the hierarchical and highly structured institutions that are traditional Catholic churches. Consequently, base Christian communities are attractive to women's activism. It should come as no surprise, therefore, that some women activists who join faith-based NGOs started their work in base Christian communities. Monreal Molina, for instance, began her activism in a base Christian community on the edge of Ciudad Juárez. Susan Eckstein (1999: 8) notes in her research that "Base Communities have been a force behind a range of movements." And the political reality along the border expands the social context for women to organize around border women's issues. When women's faith-based organizations like the Centro Mujeres de Fe y Esperanza came along, they found receptive audiences of like-minded lay and religious women.

Founded in 1993, the Centro Mujeres de Fe y Esperanza was among the first women's faith-based NGOs to emerge in the El Paso/Ciudad Juárez area. Its membership cut across ethnic lines. Ida Berresheim, a Catholic nun and one of the cofounders of the Centro, joined the group in its first year. In her recollection, the women of the Centro started by working with refugees and homeless people. From its inception, the Centro's workers and members included lay women and nuns. A number were educators and health workers. After discussing and assessing the communities in the area, the Centro's organizers decided to channel their efforts into programs focused on women's development. Berresheim recalls that, "after a time, and after soliciting funds mostly from women's [religious] congregations throughout the United States, they were able to open this place." They began to get to know the local social service agencies and formed partnerships and subsequently developed programs to train women as *promotoras de salud* (promoters of health).

The Centro is one model for women's mobilization in the region. As its mission statement states, the Centro's members, "as women on the US / Mexico border, . . . stand in solidarity with women throughout the world who actively seek peace with justice for the earth and for people." Their goal is to work together to transform the social structures that oppress or limit women. And they begin by concentrating their activism on local projects. For example, the Centro's Valores y Vida program focuses on building women's self-esteem and challenging the assumptions of traditional family structures and women's subordinate roles in them. The goal is to provide opportunities for women to discuss alternative family structures where women can be equal partners. That is why for women leaders who organize border women, raising self-esteem is paramount in the programs they offer. Over time, women identified other areas that needed attention.

For example, Centro programs addressed women's economic marginality — identifying the sources of economic exploitation and developing strategies to combat them. By challenging the Latino family structure and critiquing other social institutions, especially religious ones, Latinas, Chicanas, and Mexicanas who join these NGOS organize and increase their political mobilization. They do so promoting what we can call a nonpatriarchal, action-oriented religious spirituality as social activism. For example, women at the Centro reject church institutions that value keeping families intact but fail to confront family violence, a social problem that disproportionately affects women and children. They also question other social structures that produce economic and political marginalization. One of the characteristics of the Centro is the number of women who come from the impoverished and disenfranchised colonias. Questioning such exploitation attracts Latinas to the Centro. While its programs seek to help women transform their lives and their spirituality into activism, the Centro maximizes efforts by networking with other women's NGOs in the region. The networking has produced an active and effective cluster of organizations addressing myriad issues that border women confront.

Organizations in the El Paso/Ciudad Juárez cluster are affiliated with church groups that include Catholic women's congregations, the Jewish Women's Council of El Paso, and the YWCA, which support a wide range of human rights border issues. More specifically, interviews conducted with organizers for this study revealed that women's NGOs on the U.S.-Mexico border are linked by their local and transnational concern for women's rights and human rights broadly defined. In these sociopolitical contexts, alliances among and across women's NGOs are focused on "being together" around women's issues rather than on national divisions. The research also reveals a rich relationship between a number of women's religious groups and the grassroots organizations with which they work. For example, Sister Kathleen Erickson of the Women's Intercultural Center in Anthony came to the border because her commitment to the poor and marginalized led her to take religious vows, as a Sister of Mercy, that included working with women and children. She came with "a certain amount of awareness about the women's movement and the fact that women are disadvantaged in most areas of our society."

The decision to commit to border communities was also made by nuns outside of Erickson's religious order. Eleanor Stech, who with her fellow Adrian Dominican sister Donna Kustusch helped establish the Centro Mujeres de Fe y Esperanza in Ciudad Juárez, explained how she came to work on the border.

I think I would trace . . . my interest to our congregational meetings that we had . . . from the seventies on. We made as a congregation a deliberate choice to work for justice and peace that was really based on what was happening in the church and what was happening, especially in our consciousness on women's position — the injustice with which they are treated in our country and worldwide. We came to El Paso, we crossed over the bridge, saw what was happening in Juárez in the colonias there and . . . I decided to ask to come here and join Donna, who was already in this area, to see what we could do together.

Stech's narrative provides a context for understanding how religious, class, and ethnic boundaries were crossed in women's organizing along this stretch of the U.S.-Mexico border. Such crossings are important because "boundaries locate persons as members of a group, but it is group consciousness that imparts a larger significance to a collectivity" (Taylor and Whittier 1992: 114). Here feminist or women's consciousness and politicization created a foundation on which women's protest communities, despite their differences, came together for common causes. How they did so was told in stories of how spiritual journeys combined with justice concerns to join Latina activists in a common effort to empower border women and their communities.

The Adrian Dominican Sisters, part of an international congregation of more than one thousand women religious, are key figures in this history. Their stated mission is to discover and identify themselves as women called to share faith and life with one another, and sent into the world to be with others in promoting peace and justice. Their border mission focuses on a number of themes, including the human rights and political status of women, economic and social development, children and youth, the environment, the health and economic status of women, and education. Thus much of what women's religious organizations (like the Adrian Dominican Sisters, the Sisters of Mercy, and the Sisters of the Incarnate Word) do in El Paso/Ciudad Juárez is captured in the national sentiment of women's religious orders represented in the Leadership Conference of Women Religious (LCWR). Founded in 1956 as the Conference of Major Superiors of Women, LCWR was given canonical status in 1959 by decree of the Vatican Congregation for Institutes of Consecrated Life and Societies of Apostolic Life. This recognition by the hierarchy of the Catholic Church gave the network legitimacy and visibility in influential circles. Membership in LCWR is open to Catholic sisters who are principal administrators of their religious institutes (orders) in the United States. Of particular note for our discussion here is that the orders linked to LCWR include the Adrian Dominican

Sisters, the Sisters of Mercy, the Sisters of the Incarnate Word, and CLAR, which several women interviewed for this study described as important to their networks. All these organizations offered important support for the work of the women's NGOs in this study.

That these religious organizations formed alliances and coalitions with the NGOs discussed here shows how seemingly different women's organizations can find bases for alliances and coalitions. The missions of the women's religious organizations complemented the vision of community work that nonreligious women's NGOs adopted in Michoacán and El Paso / Ciudad Juárez. The goals of groups like LCWR coincided with and supported other groups that committed to work for a just world order by focusing on women. María de Jesús Gringas Aguirre of the Centro Mujeres Tonantzín, a Mexican Catholic Sister of the Incarnate Word, believes that "the most oppressed people, the most needy, are women, especially among the poor, the marginal, the mistreated, the humiliated. I feel a great calling to work with women. We are working to recover our dignity, our place in society, families, and churches." Gringas Aguirre's calling to work with border women reflects the spiritual journey of women who work in faith-based NGOs.

Assessing the impact of these efforts, Concha of MPD reflected that the women's movement had brought change but that "in the process of challenging institutions and pressuring for change some mistakes were made, particularly in making men feel so pressured that the potential for forming alliances was difficult." It was important, for example, to "discuss and debate with men within the church, asking them that just as they studied Marxism they should study feminism, and let's study it together." Stech saw this latter approach as producing important results for the women's movement, because she sees that new groups are forming to challenge the church to facilitate discussion of women's plight in broader circles. More important, many gender issues are being couched as global concerns or as connected to global issues. According to Stech, in Mexico, "the process for change is taking root [in rural communities] among rural women, in transforming and opening eyes around global ideas, not just feminism, but in coming together around collectives, cooperatives [many of them mixed, with men and women working together], and that already creates a different type of woman. So you come along and present proposals around gender issues, and they accept them in a heartbeat." Becoming agents of change therefore means not only deepening understanding of how women can effect systemic change but also thinking about how to increase the scope of their corporate voice through networking.

One can argue, then, that the focus women's NGOs have on poverty, racism, classism, and other ways women's oppression takes shape creates opportunities for reaching across ethnic, racial, and class boundaries. Making connections across borders, however they are defined, is a goal of global feminism. As Charlotte Bunch (1993: 251) has exhorted, "To make global feminist consciousness a powerful force in the world demands that we make the local, global and the global, local. Such a movement is not based on international travel and conferences, although these may be useful, but must be centered on a sense of connectedness among women active at the grass roots in various regions." This type of vision for community work and raising gender consciousness is coming together for women in NGOs. The point here, Concha said, is that this is also influencing women's vision of their place in their churches, which brings them to question the roots of patriarchal dominance: "We are each contributing to this process of change, each like a grain of sand."

I remember one of the first meetings we organized, "Doing Theology from the Perspective of Women." Bishop Sergio Méndez Arceo [well known for his work on human rights and one of the architects of liberation theology in the sixties and seventies] was there, and he questioned us very hard when we were done. He would say, "And so, what do you think about abortion?" And we said, "Well, it is the woman who should decide. He responded, "No, but the child," etc., etc. He was not too happy. . . . Then Sergio Méndez began to say "brothers and sisters," and then he invited a woman Protestant pastor whom we had invited to concelebrate [mass] with him. Don Sergio is an extremely open person, a beautiful person, and so this Catholic bishop invited the pastor and said that we had to say "brothers and sisters." From there the issue [of gender inclusiveness in the church] was included in other places.

Méndez Arceo's inviting a woman pastor to concelebrate mass typified a willingness by at least progressive leaders in the Catholic Church, particularly those associated with liberation theology, to accept the challenge women were bringing to them. While the bishop's mind may not have changed on the question of abortion, he showed women his support of their taking leadership in the church. For Stech and others like her, engaging, dialoguing, and debating with the leadership was important for making the alliances necessary to bring about change in their local churches. The goal from there, as feminist Christian women saw it, was to change society beginning with churches. One can question such a strategy's chances of success, but the story here is rather how the strategies women have adopted broadened their activism.

SUMMARY

We have seen in this chapter how together Catholic nuns, laity, Protestants, and members of other faith communities, both Latinas and non-Latinas, nurtured women's NGO networks in El Paso/Ciudad Juárez and Michoacán. Networking is important to successful mobilization, because as "resource mobilization and political opportunity theorists argue organization, networks, allies, the presence of a cycle of protest, and a reform atmosphere are central to the emergence and success of movements" (Cohen and Arato 1992: 550). The YWCA in El Paso and Casa Peregrina in Ciudad Juárez serve women by providing transition housing. The Jewish Women's Council identified domestic violence as a major problem in El Paso and supported the creation of the Battered Women's Shelter. La Posada, founded by a group of Catholic nuns, also provides shelter for women victims of domestic violence and their children. Mujer Obrera, not a faith-based NGO but important to the El Paso/Ciudad Juárez women's NGO network, offers political space for women to organize around labor issues. Bienestar Familiar in El Paso and the Centro para el Desarrollo Integral de la Mujer, A.C. (Center for the Complete Development of Women, or CEDIMAC) in Ciudad Juárez help women develop self-esteem, and the groups disseminate educational materials on a number of issues important to women, particularly the impact of domestic violence on children. Centro Mujeres Tonantzín (Ciudad Juárez), Centro Mujeres de Fe y Esperanza (El Paso and Ciudad Juárez), Women's Intercultural Center (Anthony, New Mexico/Texas), and Mujeres Unidas (Anthony) each have their own objectives, goals, and strategies, but their focus is empowering border women with self-help programs.

González Butrón's and EMAS's network of women's NGOs, which includes faith-based women's NGOs like the women of the Centro de Apoyo a la Salud Alternativa (Center for Support of Alternative Health, or CASA) in Michoacán, MPD, the Asociación de Pastoras, and Católicas por el Derecho a Decidir in Mexico City, follows a similar pattern to that of networks in El Paso/Ciudad Juárez. Networks are important to women's activism whether the venues are faith-based or not. But the embedding of faith-based women's networks in the women's movement is an important and often overlooked part of the movement's history. Here border women's activism shows that Latina community work engages women religious and faith communities in general. Faced with making their case against patriarchal dominance, women in Latin America and the United States formed and supported organizations with shared ideals and goals. This history underscores the international scope of the women's movement. And it encompasses a broad spectrum of women's protest communities. Given what NGOs have done to expand the women's movement into grassroots communities, they are undoubtedly a success. The next chapter focuses on the challenges they face.

CHAPTER FOUR

Are NGOs a Panacea?

Some Observations on the Future of NGOs

Events like the UN Fourth World Conference on Women in Beijing leave no doubt as to the vast potential of women's nongovernmental organizations. The narratives in this book testify that women's NGOs in Mexico and on the U.S.-Mexico border are politically and socially empowering. Through NGOs women mobilize. And the transnational mobilization efforts of women's NGOs have played "a key role in facilitating interaction and cooperation among feminist organizations" (Moghadam 2000: 61). But anyone working with or writing about NGOs would be remiss not to address the challenges they face. This chapter discusses how women's NGOs are affected by the enormous strain of chasing after money. "I have to recognize that the economic, that the financing is foremost, and that I am not good at it," admitted Dolores Leony of the Centro para el Desarrollo Integral de la Mujer, A.C. (Center for the Complete Development of Women, Inc., or CEDIMAC). Not only does the survival of NGOs require fundraising skills quite different from the community organizing that attracted most members to the movement, but more important, as this chapter will show, dependency on outside sources of funding can threaten the integrity of an NGO's mission. "If NGOs have no assets of their own, they run the risk of dependencies and even co-optations" (Staudt and Coronado 2002: 53). And the competition for grants is a source of strain within the organizations in other ways. Funding can create conflict as paid staff exercises greater influence in decisions than unpaid staff. Internal conflicts also emerge as decisions are made on who gets to travel to meetings, particularly abroad. Those who travel have default decision-making authority, becoming spokespeople for the organization. How can financial pressures undermine the sisterhood many consider to be central to global feminism? Do these limitations outweigh the benefits of women's activism in NGOs?

WHAT HANGING BY A FINANCIAL THREAD CAN MEAN

Some women's groups spend a lot of their time thinking about where the next grant will come from as they try to sustain projects. For example, Bienestar Familiar of El Paso, which focuses on health issues, receives most of its funding from a Paso del Norte Health Foundation grant and a smaller amount from a group of nuns associated with the Centro Mujeres de Fe y Esperanza. The goal of the Paso del Norte Health Foundation is to improve the health and wellness of the almost 2 million residents of the El Paso/ Ciudad Juárez region through education and prevention. With $130 million in assets from the sale of Providence Memorial Hospital in 1995, Paso del Norte is one of the largest private foundations on the U.S.-Mexico border. Through grants the foundation supports Bienestar Familiar and other NGOs that focus on education and health. Bienestar Familiar has received grants to promote the Paso del Norte initiative "Healthy Communities." The problem for Bienestar Familiar is that although it is considered a community-based group that identifies projects for foundations, it is vulnerable to the grant cycles administered by funding agencies like Paso del Norte. The first three-year grant for the "Healthy Communities" program ended in 2000. Since then, Bienestar Familiar has expanded its work to collaborations with HUD (Housing and Urban Development) and receives small grants from a number of foundations, including the Jessie Smith Noyes Foundation and Ms., among others. But the grants are small.

NGO leaders noted that funders solicit little if any input from NGOs. The relationships tend to be top-bottom where NGOs submit proposals for grants under initiatives set by the granting agencies or foundations, which set the agenda for what will be funded. As an example, the Rockefeller Foundation's Web site advertises a strategy called "Global Inclusion," which supports work on policy issues at regional and global levels that must relate to, and advance, the goals of the Rockefeller Foundation. Similarly, the Ford Foundation seeks to strengthen democratic values, reduce poverty and injustice, promote international cooperation, and advance human achievement. But the Ford Foundation also makes clear to those seeking funding that it directs its support to activities that are within its current interests and that it believes will have wide impact. Consequently, when NGOs "continuously apply for grants, their missions are sometimes distorted as they respond to requests for proposals developed by funders: private foundations and corporations, government agencies and international agencies" (Staudt and Coronado 2002: 53).

Because of these challenges, Bernadette Habur of La Posada in El Paso noted, some groups develop multiple funding strategies.

> We do not do government money; all our monies are private donations and from grants that we write. . . . One of the reasons we haven't used government money is simply the red tape is so much. Even with United Way, there's a degree of red tape, and believe it or not sometimes those monies are not real secure. We've had pretty good fortune in writing grants. . . . We have a good reputation. But our grants sometimes come from here, locally, and from within the state, and we have gotten grants from outside the state, but not as often as from within the state, because granting foundations can be limiting.

Habur added that when it comes to foundations, the funds are earmarked with "emphasis on social work, homeless people, homeless women, children, education, that type of thing." For women's faith-based organizations like La Posada funding from religious groups provides the group some degree of freedom to do its own work. Donna Kustusch of the Centro Mujeres de Fe y Esperanza in Ciudad Juárez noted that

> Our money really basically comes from religious-oriented foundations in the United States. . . . It's year-by-year funding. It's difficult. Those are

always difficult questions for us. Basically our goal is to enable leadership so that the women can have a sense of themselves, and we've got a long way to go on that because funding-wise we are at the point now where next year I'm hoping to more formally establish some kind of legal entity for this. I think women here are trained enough now . . . about how to write grants and to find our own funding.

The social services orientation of some NGOs makes them better positioned to receive financial support from outside sources. The YWCA in El Paso is a good example. The U.S. Department of Housing and Urban Development funded the YWCA to confront housing issues in El Paso. "My job is to match the funds," said Florence Buchmueller, "so I get it from local foundations, community development block grant money from the city, emergency shelter grant money, because we're still considered a shelter. Women can stay here up to two years while emergency shelters have stricter rules, but [the residents are] still in transition, so it's supportive housing, and we're still considered a homeless shelter. I don't tell the women they're homeless, but when I go out for money, I say 'homeless.'" Buchmueller's job is made easier by the fact that in "the last few years we've had an 85 percent success rate, and the women who left us left with jobs and apartments."

THE PROBLEM WITH EXTERNAL FUNDING DEPENDENCY

But as I noted earlier, the problem with funding is the time NGOs spend talking about and planning for it. NGOs are forced to compete against each other. Maruja González Butrón of the Equipo de Mujeres en Acción Solidaria (Team of Women United in Action, or EMAS) noted the challenge that she and others faced in trying to get beyond the financial interests. "We are involved in the effort to build something real solid, interrelations among the NGOs, for mutual support and exchange, and at the same time find ways to be funded, given the difficult situation we're facing as NGOs. Working together on collaborative projects is recognized as important, because everyone sees the destructive potential in competing for funds. Not so much in Michoacán, but in Mexico City, for example, the competition is there." González Butrón and others recognize that competition for funds can destroy network relationships and undermine the support NGOs can give one another.

To address the problem, Michoacán NGOs have banded together in seeking funding. Part of the strategy has been to develop cooperative projects and propose them to funding agencies and foundations. "In many ways this is progress," said González Butrón. "Before, a lot of groups were jealous of those that were funded, and it was always just a one-way relationship between those groups and the agencies that funded them. I believe that has changed a lot." NGOs try to support each other in other ways, particularly in sharing access to computers, fax machines, and photocopiers. Still, the most typical sources of support are international funding agencies.

We [EMAS] basically survive with donations, grants from funding agencies, especially from Germany and Holland. Holland supported us for a long time through NOVIB [Nederlandse Organisatie voor Internationale Bijstand, or Netherlands Organization for International Aid] and other small funding groups, and then from Germany, for three years, through organizations supporting events like the International Prayer Day for Women. More recently we have received funds from Bread for the World and from a Canadian group called Peace and Development. These are the primary sources of funding for us. Last year we were able to get some funds for a small project from SEDESOL.[1]

Other grants come from small groups, in some cases church groups looking to support community projects.

One initiative supported raising the literacy rate for women in Michoacán. The initiative started with only three thousand dollars in support from the Comisión Evangélica Latinoamericana de Educación Cristiana (Latin American Evangelical Commission for Christian Education, or CELADEC) for what EMAS called the "Cartilla Lupe" literacy program. González Butrón noted that other NGOs supported the literacy program by "donating paper or mimeographs so we could reproduce materials."

For the few NGOs that are faith-based organizations, funding can come from organizations like CELADEC and from other religious groups. According to María de Jesús Gringas Aguirre of Centro Mujeres Tonantzín in Ciudad Juárez,

We [Centro Mujeres Tonantzín] received our primary support from our congregation [the Sisters of Charity of the Incarnate Word]. It is a fund made available for initiating missions, for the house, the office, and for start-up. After that we have done some projects with the support that we have from the [local Catholic] dioceses. We have a small subsidy as a group that does pastoral work with women in the [Ciudad Juárez] peripheral parishes, particularly for our work with women in prison. And we have had projects that have been funded from outside Mexico.

But even accepting funding from religious organizations entails risks, since such funding is not free of religious ideology, particularly as it impacts women's issues. This is why women's NGOs are eager to legalize their autonomy by forming 501C3s or *asociaciones civiles* (civil associations, as NGOs are known legally in Mexico). In talking about the establishment of the Women's Intercultural Center, Sister Kathleen Erickson emphasized how imperative it was for the center to become an NGO. "We formed a 501C3 nonprofit corporation. We are not affiliated with the diocese, or our religious community, or the church. It [the Women's Intercultural Center] is a free-standing nonprofit 501C3." But the rush to form NGOs as legal entities only solves some issues. Finding funding remains a constant nag.

The story of funding typically includes frustration such as that described by Rocío Suárez of Comunicación Intercambio y Desarrollo Humano en América Latina (Communication, Exchange, and Human Development in Latin America, or CIDHAL), a group from Cuernavaca with ties to EMAS in Michoacán.

We still have financial problems, financial and human resources. That's where we are. . . . CIDHAL has had key funding from international cooperatives for development and from ecumenical communities, with support mostly from Europe, mainly NGOs like NOVIB, church organizations like Bread for the World, and Oxfam in England. These are the basic three. But . . . right now, we are proposing basic ways to develop self-financing that includes renting space, for example, from this space here [CIDHAL's office property in Cuernavaca]. . . . We also charge for some services, for literature on health, even though that is limited and has only generated about 5 percent in income.

In organization after organization, the testimonies are similar. Why do women's NGOs find it difficult to generate funds from the very communities they serve? This question is particularly important considering the strings often attached to grants from outsiders. Some NGO leaders' answer to the question lies in the women's movement and its standing in most communities.

Yadira Cira Gómez, a university student and EMAS member who headed the Taller Permanente de Estudios de la Mujer of the Escuela de Mujeres at the Universidad Michoacana San Nicolás de Hidalgo, explained why she thought it is so hard for women's NGOs to fund their own activities.

Today, I believe the women's movement is very small. At least, the movement is very small at the regional [more local] level. It isn't widely spread. It suffered a great decline after the 1980s. The feminist perspective didn't really catch on, and now I think we are suffering a bit from the criticisms that were made of the feminist movement in the 1970s, because little is known of what it means to talk about gender. . . . So yes, a lot has changed in what the feminist movement is, but it is like it has not really achieved much in having a real place in the broader [poor people's] social movements here.

González Butrón added to Cira Gómez's observation by noting the disconnect between an academic women's movement and a grassroots women's movement.

There are very privileged spaces at the academic level. Research projects that are very interesting, very important; but these efforts, we feel them still to be very disconnected from the larger women's movement. Consequently, one of the areas of work for us in the group [EMAS] has been how to bridge all of this [the work with grassroots women], to stimulate making connections. So, we have produced two pamphlets for our series *Pensamiento y lucha (Thought and Struggle)* that try to vindicate the role of women in Mexican history. It was the thesis of Esperanza Tuñón, a professor of sociology. We felt that her work could not just stay in the library of the UNAM [Universidad Nacional Autónoma de México].

González Butrón saw EMAS's publication of Tuñón's thesis as a strategy to bridge two groups of women: those who come from privileged backgrounds and grassroots women, who are also part of the history of the women's movement.

CONFLICT AND COMPETITION UNDERMINE NGOS

In addition to disjunctures among social movements, women's NGOs must confront competition among them. Patricia Monreal Molina of the Organización Popular Independiente (Popular Independent Organization, or OPI) in Ciudad Juárez noted that when NGOs try to coordinate activities conflicts can emerge because the various NGOs want to emphasize different issues or have different approaches to organizing. In talking about women's NGOs in greater El Paso/Ciudad Juárez, she used the crisis around the murders of women in the Juárez desert to illustrate how difficult coordinating efforts can be. "We tried to organize what we wanted to call a coordination of women's organizations. Well, there we had a lot of battles, because with all the different foci and the like, it made it difficult. In the end we succeeded in some things." The NGOs were able to pressure the local government to be more aggressive in investigating the murders. The efforts led to the creation of a Ciudad Juárez agency for sexual crimes. Despite these successes, Monreal Molina saw reason for concern.

In general, I believe, there are deficiencies in the NGOs. It is difficult to coordinate efficiently, because where do you begin. . . . In other words, you have to come up with proposals, ideas, and then yes, . . . there have been problems with a coordinated strategy [to bring attention to the murders]. But it has been only about being in constant protest, protest, protest. And still the crimes and those things kept happening and even increased. We didn't have a strategy about what other work to do.

In the end, Monreal Molina found comfort in the fact that attention to the murders "helped give birth to a project to build a crisis center that came to be called Casa Amiga [Friendship House]."

But each new collaborative project that NGOs generate takes time away from an individual NGO's own work. Collaborative efforts can become a source of conflict and tension, Monreal Molina said. "While some may want to focus exclusively on the violence and the murders, others of us want to work on other things. . . . for a number of us we have other strategies focused on prevention. What has happened with the coordination effort, with the creation of Casa Amiga? The base for coordination has all come from within Casa Amiga. In the end, you weaken one thing to strengthen another." The concern expressed shows that an individual NGO's objectives may get lost in the shuffle when it joins collaborative efforts.

The expansion of CIDHAL into other organizing efforts is a case in point. CIDHAL's extension to Mexico City was viewed by some as a strain on the group's personnel, space, and focus. Almost from the start, the two groups within CIDHAL began to operate separately. Former member Itziar Lozano noted that

> The rhythm in the provinces is very different: things go slower, and also social movements in the provinces in the seventies in Cuernavaca and Morelos more generally had been severely repressed. Because of these differences, the work in Cuernavaca was more autonomous, slower, with less pressure, but less focused, more difficult to grasp and consolidate as a force. By contrast here [in Mexico City] the demands were very strong from the beginning and the nexus with the popular movements were much stronger, clearer, and the demands much more explicit. We started working with women who were already organized via the popular movements. That is where we gained our strength.

At first, the two CIDHAL groups worked in tandem and without much incident. That all changed after the 1985 earthquake in Mexico City, which altered the nature of the work people were doing in the capital, primarily because of the social needs that the disaster created.

In Mexico City CIDHAL began providing services that the state could not. "There was a lot of energy put into those efforts that sustained work with the *colonias*," Lozano said, "with the organizations supported by people there." But in the aftermath of the earthquake, women who once worked together formed new organizations. For example, Mujeres en Acción Sindical (Women for Union Action) became its own NGO after splitting from CIDHAL. New NGOs proliferated, often started by people who worked in one NGO like CIDHAL and then moved on to create others. In the end, CIDHAL faced an internal crisis, which Lozano described as "very painful."

Since 1991, there's been a lot of change. The group had gotten too big; later it diminished in size, partly because of problems internal to the group, partly because of changes in the focus of the group's projects, and partly because of financing problems. . . . There started to be strong conflicts among the women who had been working with popular groups, who were members of CIDHAL and who wanted to raise more radical issues, more class-based issues. We came to disagree over the seminars on public politics. A group of very radical women [within CIDHAL] in the end came to take over the process and later the group until they took over the center.

Because of the tensions and the split, Lozano left CIDHAL in 1992. For her, there were too many differences over the work and the direction that CIDHAL in Cuernavaca had taken. Today, CIDHAL continues to operate as a feminist NGO providing educational alternatives and services to empower women.

BUILDING FINANCIAL SUPPORT AND STRATEGIES FOR THE FUTURE

The testimonies show that conflict over funding is one of the greatest obstacles that NGOs face. Some funding agencies and foundations have documented the frustration in surveys with NGO leaders. NOVIB conducted such surveys in 1997 and 2002. Respondents reacted to fifty-three statements about NOVIB-sponsored efforts. The responses underscore the tensions between NGOs and the groups that fund them. NGO leaders said funders needed to conduct more field visits to better understand the needs of NGOs rather than imposing priorities on them from afar and to be more open to the ones set by the NGOs themselves. Almost a quarter of respondents considered NOVIB too bureaucratic in relating to NGOs (Oxfam NOVIB 2002).

NGO leaders interviewed for this book found that NGOs have little power to influence organizational priorities when they look for financial support outside the group. Instead, funders can dictate NGO agendas. This inhibits

NGOs as social movement organizations with their own visions and goals. Because of the tenuous relations with funding agencies and foundations, Lozano noted that Red entre Mujeres, the group she was affiliated with at the time of her interview for this book, was created to better collaboration among women's NGOs, specifically in their exchange of information about funders. "Not so much for developing sensibilities, but [for] systematizing information, analyzing and debating it to put forth strategies to work for all of them. The main objective was to strengthen the NGOs and strengthen the movement." The challenge for the Red is how to secure funds and yet remain true to the objectives of the women's movement.

According to Lozano, in a 1989 meeting of Red entre Mujeres held in Montevideo, Uruguay, "women's organizations gathered . . . to question their relations to funders, how much to cooperate. There was a lot of consensus . . . in questioning the concept of a movement and the link to funders." Lozano added that "there [in Montevideo] we also began to clarify what it meant to strengthen the feminist and gender perspectives of the NGOs. [We began] to be more firm with relation to sources of funding." Three years after the Montevideo gathering, at another Red meeting, Magaly Pineda of the Centro de Investigación para la Acción Femenina (Center for Research on Women's Action, or CIPAF, in the Dominican Republic) urged that the agenda of the Red include direct discussions with NOVIB representatives. Lozano summed up the meeting:

> Together with counterparts from NOVIB, committees were formed that called for women's platforms. . . . We discussed our situation, our institutional status, expressed our need to strengthen our organizations, the difficulties we faced in dealing with funders, and other things related to our various projects. . . . There the sense of needing to establish much broader relations with the funders emerged, even though we had not yet been able to formalize or make clear what putting political pressure on them meant.

The Red meetings proved fruitful. NOVIB agreed to conduct a study on the level of satisfaction between NGOs and funding agencies, beginning with a focus on NOVIB itself in order to assess better the extent of the problem.

The Red is an example of an NGO that has succeeded in making its funders more sensitive to it and its needs. The discussions with NOVIB brought into the open the problems funders can pose for NGOs, even unintentionally. The efforts of Red entre Mujeres show that mobilizing women's NGO networks at international forums can generate discussion, debate, and the sharing of information to address difficult issues. As Gonzálcz Butrón of EMAS noted,

> Fur a number of years, we believed that it would be more effective to concentrate on fortifying local and even state-level groups and organizations. But at this moment I believe that it is fundamental to link with other organizations in the region, at national as well as international levels. It seems to me that it is central that our NGOs begin to work on developing international platforms, with our own proposals. One of my dreams is to connect local groups to other levels. But not all of us have the same opportunity to travel, to link ourselves to other groups.

On a more practical level, for a number of NGOs, networks allow the exchange of information and facilitate locating funding for collaborative projects.

Crediting European women's NGOs for their support of third world women's NGOs, Lozano noted: "There have been European funding agencies that after being pressured by women's groups there have supported women's groups throughout the third world. . . . We have had [Europeans] who came and told us, 'We learned that you are doing work with women. We want to know if you have some project or other things going on, because we have a mandate to look for your projects to finance them.'" But even here there can be tensions with what third world women's groups call the "North-South" divide. According to Lozano (1994), this is really a dynamic between first and third world NGOs, where the latter feel they have to fight for the ability to define their own needs and ways to address them. The goal is to "find alternatives that allow one to sustain . . . one's own agenda, which is for now one of the principal challenges for the women's and feminist movements today" (ibid.). As this book has shown, Latinas in Mexico and the U.S. Southwest are searching for those alternatives.

CHAPTER FIVE

Despite Limitations Women's NGOs Push Forward

This book began with a community activist at a feminist forum who asked about the meaning of the word *feminismo*. As she noted, and as the grass-roots women's NGOs in this study strived to accomplish in empowering women to activism, feminist visions can indeed begin with developing "fe-en-mi-mismo," or faith in oneself. Doing so has led grassroots women in Mexico and on the U.S.-Mexico border to embrace women's issues linking them to larger community concerns. For some, engagement in women-centered activism grew out of community work in *colonias*, or in organizing around labor, violence against women, migrants' rights, AIDS, the environment, or political representation. This led women's NGOs to form coalitions and alliances with other groups and movements as part of their organizing strategies. Women crossed any number of class, race, and geographical boundaries to do women-centered community work locally, nationally, and internationally.

Key to NGOs' ability to pursue their objectives were networks where collaboration alleviated financial limitations and where shared personnel and expertise made it easier to organize events and provide services. Networks also created opportunities for dialogue and the exchange of ideas as NGOs strategized to advance women's issues and programs that empower women. Networks often provided the base from which organizers could connect to the world of funding and learn how to balance the pursuit of funding with faithfulness to organizational missions and goals. By studying two activist women's communities, Michoacán and El Paso/Ciudad Juárez, we have seen how such communities work on behalf of women even when activists adopt different strategies. Despite differences in approach, women's activist communities often have more in common than not. Latinas on the U.S.-Mexico border and in the Mexican interior highlighted the way global capitalism affects people's daily lives, particularly those of women, and the fact that people are mobilizing, despite the odds, against such forces.

The successes of these two women's activist communities cannot easily be quantified. But grassroots women have challenged women's activism and feminism in particular and changed them forever. In both Michoacán and El Paso/Ciudad Juárez, two communities where prior to the 1990s there was minimal women's organizing, women's activism has flourished and become very visible. The success and impact of this organizing could be seen when the Ciudad Juárez government was pressured into attending to the murders of and violence against women and into supporting the creation of a women's crisis center, Casa Amiga. There are now more homeless shelters and domestic crisis centers for women in El Paso, and they work together and refer women to each other, whether they are the YWCA, Centro Mujeres de Fe y Esperanza, or others discussed in this book. La Mujer Obrera in El Paso, whose history goes back further than most of the NGOs in this study, now counts on other women's organizations to help it bring attention to women's labor concerns as part of broader human rights issues in a region where once La Mujer Obrera was the only voice. Women's voices, as represented by organizations like the Centro de Servicios Municipales Heriberto Jara (CESEM), Mujeres por la Democracia, and the Nación Purépecha, are now central to the Michoacán political scene as well. Nación Purépecha is particularly important, as indigenous communities in Mexico only recently have come into their own politically, and indigenous women are emerging as central figures in the movement.

The sociopolitical nuances differentiating women's activist communities in Michoacán and greater El Paso/Ciudad Juárez enable a rich cross-cultural understanding of social movement organizations as they struggle on particular turfs. Both local and global politics influenced why the women's NGOs came into being, what shaped their goals and strategies, and why and how they clustered in networks. But we have also found common threads in women's activist communities and how they focus their commitments to raising women's consciousness in order to empower them to action. Maruja González Butrón of EMAS summarized it best:

> I believe that the most efficient way that we have found convergence with the various women's organizations is by realizing we have more that unites us than divides us. And also by working together in various ways, as pressure groups, whether focusing on the state or on tactics pushing any number of our objectives. There is much that we [in NGOs] have to say because we have accumulated years of experience and practice that are very close to the lives of grassroots women; these now are bearing fruit in the way these women's groups are exerting their voice. . . . I believe this is an area where we are gaining strength.

If you consider where grassroots women's groups were prior to the 1970s, at the height of what historically is identified as the second wave of feminism in both Mexico and the United States, Latina women's NGOs have come a long way. Grassroots and third world women's groups have gone from virtual nonexistence to shaping women's and feminist discourses.

The first steps in this evolution could be seen in June 1975, when the United Nations convened its first global conference on women in Mexico City (United Nations 2002). As documents presented by the UN Division for the Advancement of Women show, the 1975 World Conference on Women, part of the International Women's Year, marked the beginning of a process that cast public women's issues as human rights issues. By the late 1970s, the UN Commission on the Status of Women had woven itself into the United Nations' global political agenda. The UN meetings spotlighted grassroots women's issues that would nurture international exchange and activism in the following decades. The international meetings heightened awareness of issues particularly relevant to grassroots women. The United Nations' taking up women's issues would come to have a global impact for women's NGOs and women's activism as the Fourth World Conference on Women showed in 1995. The Beijing conference showcased grassroots women's activism and its globally oriented feminist platforms.

The UN efforts impelled what would become an ongoing international campaign for the implementation, promotion, and protection of women's human rights. These efforts have particularly emphasized the elimination of violence against women. It is no accident that the interviews for this book, whether in Michoacán or El Paso/Ciudad Juárez, articulated the NGOs' focus on this cause. Women's NGOs have stressed connecting women's public and private lives, including all forms of sexual harassment, exploitation, and trafficking of women. In highlighting violence against women, these NGOs have testified for the rights of women and against patriarchal practices that promote cultural prejudices. These practices include religious extremism, which has harmed women throughout the world and indirectly supported forms of violence against them (United Nations 2002). The feminist scholar Chanda Talpade Mohanty (2003: 235) notes:

> It is especially on the bodies and lives of women and girls from the Third World/South — the Two Third Worlds — that global capitalism writes its script, and it is by paying attention to and theorizing the experiences of these communities of women and girls that we demystify capitalism as a system of debilitating sexism and racism and envision anticapitalist resistance. Thus any analysis of the effects of globalization needs to centralize the experiences and struggles of these particular communities of women and girls.

The narratives of women NGO leaders in this book call for a grounding of feminist visions by incorporating grassroots women's contributions into them. Already women's NGOs have shown that rallying around issues of violence against women as a violation of human rights helps to bring women from different parts of the women's movement together to spur organizing efforts and for dialogue across women's communities.

In addition, we also learn from women interviewed for this book that women's NGOs and specific struggles for connecting health, education, social, political, economic, and environmental concerns to human rights is an important contribution of grassroots women's activism. The narratives provided in this book are food for dialogue on the question posed by Mohanty (2003: 237): "What does it mean to make antiglobalization [of capitalism] a key factor for feminist theorizing and struggle?" Or, put another way, how can activists begin to shape strategies that center women's struggles squarely on the negative consequences of global capitalism for women and their broader communities? The activist communities in Michoacán and greater El Paso/Ciudad Juárez show women's communities and feminist scholars in particular how collective action can be grounded to achieve common objectives. As the sociologist Alberto Melucci (1995: 43) put it, "purposive orientation constructed by means of social relationships" gives sense to the advantages of women's communities' working toward common goals. Opportunities for exchange and networking, however big or small, whether global or local, allow women to maximize participation and contribute to a broader women's movement.

As Dolores Leony of the Centro para el Desarrollo Integral de la Mujer, A.C. (CEDIMAC), in Ciudad Juárez noted:

> For me, at a personal level, I feel enriched by the relations with them [other NGOs]. It makes us feel like . . . we have no borders that women have to relate to one another, not only at local levels but nationally, and also with others across the river. It helps to learn more on how to work across groups. I have gone to visit the El Paso Rape Crisis Center and the Battered Women's Shelter. These linkages have been important.

Patricia Monreal Molina of Organización Popular Independiente (OPI) in Ciudad Juárez added, "I believe there have been great gains. It seems to me that women's organizations in general are right on with regard to their focus on women's issues and the alternatives they have to offer." Imelda García of Bienestar Familiar observed that the women's movement

> has opened a lot of doors and made people really talk about things that a lot of people didn't want to talk about. . . . I think as women together we have so many things in common and that we can really, really work together to make the changes needed, but I think that there has to be more dialogue, because there are some differences and those are just the realities. . . . What I see on the border is something that I have struggled with all my life: how to balance values. Sometimes you get insecure in your belief systems, because people tell you that there is a better way to do things and so you are constantly living with one foot on each side, and I relate to that a lot. I may have gotten educated, but it's something I still

struggle with every day. . . . I think in working with [border community] programs trying not to lose the people is so important, because that is so much a part of who you are, and so I feel closely tied to the women I work with on both sides of the border.

For González Butrón, the connection with grassroots communities is perhaps the greatest accomplishment of the women's movement and may be where our feminist futures lie, "We have found spaces for women from diverse backgrounds to work together. We have a lot more we work on that brings us together than divides us now. . . . We now say we have moved from protests to proposals. There is a lot we've accomplished. It has been years of accumulated experiences and practices that are now closer and more meaningful to women's everyday lives." For González Butrón and others these connections give greater meaning to their activism and what they articulate in striving for global feminism. These links underscore the importance of mobilizing around grassroots women's issues for understanding how women, whether indigenous, poor, educated, Latina or not, can come together to fight for women's rights as human rights.

The women interviewed for this book applaud the fact that women's movements today are developing strategies for transcending, shaping, and crossing political and ethnic boundaries through grassroots activism. This study shows it can be done through forging alliances and coalitions across women's communities. Others are coming to the same conclusions. Kathleen Staudt and Irasema Coronado (2002: 170), for example, note that "despite daunting obstacles, we identified cases of cross-border collaborations and coalition building." And "these success stories connect local people and organizations to regional, national, and international organizations." This is critical, for as Mohanty (2003: 250) put it, "a transnational feminist practice depends on building feminist solidarities across the divisions of place, identity, class, work, belief, and so on. In these fragmented times it is both very difficult to build these alliances and also never more important to do so. Global capitalism both destroys the possibilities and also offers up new ones." This book speaks to and enriches a growing body of feminist scholarship that shows the potential in global and transnational feminist approaches to activism.

The women's movement has grown in that women-centered, community-based activism is underscoring that "community is created in and through struggles . . . as well as through casual interactions with people who share some aspects of [the communities'] daily lives" (Naples 1998: 337). This is important, because "as a dynamic process, the social construction of community offers the possibility for redefinition of boundaries, for broadened constituencies, and for seemingly unlikely alliances" (ibid.). Today, the experiences Latinas have and the work they do in NGOs not only broaden feminist discourses but create a space for the *chispa*, the spark or passion, of women's politics to become a flame. Such commitments require a more global and transnational view of the women's movement. Latinas' grassroots communities are breaking new ground for feminist and women-centered activism and are showing us how we can envision and work toward new feminist futures.

Notes

Quotations from primary and secondary sources have been translated from the Spanish by the author.

INTRODUCTION

1. I use *Latina* throughout this book to refer to women of Latin American descent. Lara Medina (2004: 153) notes that it "is an umbrella term that does not do justice to the diversity and complexity of specific Latino groups but implies a stance of solidarity with marginalized peoples of Latin American descent." Elsewhere in this book, the terms *Chicana*, *Chicano*, and *Mexican American* refer to people of Mexican descent in U.S.-Mexican border communities in the context of U.S. history. More specifically, *Chicana* refers to women of Mexican ancestry born in the United States "with political awareness and ethnic pride that emerged during the civil rights struggles of the 1960s and 1970s" (Medina 2004: 153). Interview subjects and the U.S. Census Bureau refer to peoples of Mexican and Latin American ancestry as "Hispanics." But this term is often contested precisely because it emphasizes a cultural identification of Latin Americans with the historical narratives of Spanish conquest, subordinating the indigenous and African cultures also present in Latin America. It appears in this book only in quotations.

2. In using the term *global feminism*, I recognize that "globally, women are becoming conscious of their positions inside of the sexual-caste system within which they live. Their responses to this realization are as varied as the women who create them" (Sandoval 1990: 68). Another dimension of global feminism is the recognition of commitments "to sustain partnerships with ever-expanding allies who use policy to connect gender to virtually every principle and issue discussed in international and national arenas" (Staudt 1997: ix).

3. As Alvarez (1997: 60) notes, *base* as used here refers to grassroots or poor people's movements that use class-based politics of protest to promote grassroots survival efforts. These efforts are often referred to in Latin American studies literature as the struggles of the popular sector. According to Daniel Levine (1986: 6), "popular," base, or grassroots groups constitute the masses in social sectors oppressed or exploited by an economic social system. At a minimum, *popular* involves some notion of subordination and inequality. *Popular, base,* or *grassroots* also imply a sense of collective identity and direct attention to the ideas, beliefs, practices, and conditions of poor people, however defined, and by extension to ties that bind them to institutions of power, privilege, and meaning, as well as to their organized responses. Throughout the book *base* refers to a number of "popular," "grassroots," or poor people's movements and the class, race, and, more recently, gender-based struggles that become the foundation of their organizing.

4. CEBs, originally meant to meet the needs of observant Catholics in areas where priests were scarce, became a forum for political organizing. This is partly explained by the fact that these communities were constituted by popular groups. Phillip Berryman (1987: 68) has concluded that in the 1960s "the 'basic Christian communities' had arisen out of a critical awareness of the inadequacy of existing pastoral models, the results of some earlier pastoral efforts based on small groups, initial experiments in a number of countries, and a rationale supplied by theologians and sociologists."

5. My discussion of the U.S.-Mexico borderlands builds on "analyses of border transgressions that emphasize contemporary diasporic practices of hybrid place-making and non-absolutist citizenship" (Sadowski-Smith 2002: 2). More specifically, I rely on the notion of the U.S.-Mexico borderlands as a site "where conflicts between oppressive structures of the nation-state and globalization, on the one hand, and emerging alternative notions of societal membership, on the other, are currently being re-articulated in a variety of oppositional forms and strategies that encompass politically constructed affiliations and cross-cultural alliances" (ibid.: 3).

6. Founded in 1929 and initially based in Texas, LULAC quickly expanded throughout the Southwest. It is now a national organization that represents the political interests of Latinos and Latinas. But within LULAC obtaining equal rights for women has taken decades, a struggle exemplified by the rise of Belén Robles as the organization's first woman president.

7. Interview by José Estrada, Oral Histories Archives, University of Texas, El Paso, April 26–27, 1976.

8. Interview by Mario T. García, Oral Histories Archives, University of Texas, El Paso, November 3, 1982.

9. This informant requested anonymity; "Graciela" is a pseudonym.

1. MICHOACÁN

1. Cities and dates of interviews are given in the list of Interviews with Leaders of Nongovernmental Organizations in the book's front matter.

2. GREATER EL PASO / CIUDAD JUÁREZ

1. This informant requested anonymity; "Graciela" is a pseudonym.

4. ARE NGOS A PANACEA?

1. The Mexican government's Subsecretaría de Desarrollo Social y Humano (Subsecretariat for Social and Human Development).

Bibliography

Alvarez, Sonia E. 1997. Contradictions of a "Women's Space" in a Male Dominant State: The Political Role of the Commissions on the Status of Women in Post-authoritarian Brazil. In *Women, International Development, and Politics: The Bureaucratic Mire*, ed. Kathleen Staudt, 59–100. Philadelphia: Temple University Press.

Anzaldúa, Gloria. 1999. *Borderlands/La Frontera: The New Mestiza*. San Francisco: Aunt Lute.

Aquino, María Pilar. 1992. *Nuestro clamor por la vida: Teología latinoamericana desde la perspectiva de la mujer*. San Juan, Costa Rica: DEI.

Baden, Sally, and Anne Marie Goetz. 1997. Who Needs [Sex] When You Can Have [Gender]? Conflicting Discourses on Gender at Beijing. In *Women, International Development, and Politics: The Bureaucratic Mire*, ed. Kathleen Staudt, 37–58. Philadelphia: Temple University Press.

Behar, Ruth, and Deborah Gordon, eds. 1995. *Women Writing Culture*. Berkeley: University of California Press.

Berryman, Phillip. 1987. *Liberation Theology: Essential Facts about the Revolutionary Movement in Latin America and Beyond*. New York: Pantheon.

Bunch, Charlotte. 1993. Prospects for Global Feminism. In *Feminist Frameworks*, ed. Allison M. Jaggar and Paula S. Rothenberg (3rd. ed.) 249–52. New York: McGraw-Hill.

Carrillo, Roxanna. 1990. Feminist Alliances: A View from Peru. In *Bridges of Power: Women's Multicultural Alliances*, ed. Lisa Albrecht and Rose M. Brewer, 199–205. Philadelphia: New Society.

City of El Paso, Department of Economic Development. 2002. El Paso Profile and Economic Summary. www.ci.el-paso.tx.us. Accessed January 4, 2002.

Cohen, Jean L., and Andrew Arato. 1992. *Civil Society and Political Theory*. Cambridge, Mass.: MIT Press.

Collins, Patricia Hill. 2000. *Black Feminist Thought: Knowledge, Consciousness, and the Politics of Empowerment*. New York: Routledge.

Conferencia Latinoamerica de Religiosos (CLAR). 1972. *La religiosa hoy en América Latina*. Bogotá: Secretariado General de la CLAR.

Coordinadora de la Region Centro. 1994. *Hacia la IV Conferencia mundial sobre la mujer en Pekín (hoy Beijing)*. Guadalajara, Jalisco: Coordinadora de la Region Centro, July. EMAS archives.

Cotera, Martha. 1977. *The Chicana feminist*. Austin: Information Systems Development.

Coyle, Laurie, Gail Hershatter, and Emily Honig. 2001. Farah Strike. www.tsha .utexas.edu/handbook/online/articles/view/FF/oef2.html. Accessed June 4, 2002.

Eckstein, Susan. 1999. Globalization and Mobilization: Civil Society Resistance to the New World Order. Paper presented at American Sociological Association Annual Conference, Chicago, August.

Equipo de Mujeres en Acción Solidaria (EMAS). 1994. *Las mujeres en Michoacán: Situación actual y propuestas*. Morelia, Michoacán, June. EMAS archives.

Espinosa Damián, Gisela, and Alma Rosa Sánchez Olvera. 1992. Feminismo y Movimientos de Mujeres en Mexico: 1970–1990. *Cuadernos para la Mujer: Pensamiento y Luchas* 7: 1–39.

Fernández-Kelly, María Patricia. 1984. *For We Are Sold, I and My People: Women and Industry in Mexico's Frontier*. Albany, N.Y.: State University of New York Press.

Ferraro, Barbara, and Patricia Hussey. 1990. *No Turning Back: Two Nuns' Battle with the Vatican over Women's Right to Choose*. New York: Poseidon.

Fregoso, Rosa Linda. 2003. *meXicana encounters: The Making of Social Identities on the Borderlands*. Berkeley: University of California Press.

Garcia, Alma M. 1989. The Development of Chicana Feminist Discourse, 1970–1980. *Gender and Society*. 3: 217–38.

Garcia, Alma M., ed. 1997. *Chicana Feminist Thought*. New York: Routledge.

Gutiérrez, Gustavo. 1973. *A Theology of Liberation*. New York: Orbis.

Hardy-Fanta, Carol. 1993. *Latina Politics, Latino Politics: Gender, Culture, and Political Participation in Boston*. Philadelphia: Temple University Press.

Hondagneu-Sotelo, Pierrette. 2001. *Domestica: Immigrant Workers Cleaning and Caring in the Shadows of Affluence*. Berkeley: University of California Press.

Hunt, Mary E., and Frances Kissling. 1987. The New York Times Ad: A Case Study in Religious Feminism. *Journal of Feminist Studies in Religion* 3(1): 115–27.

Kriesi, Hanspeter, Ruud Koopsman, Jan Willem Duyvendak, and Marco Guigni. 1995. *New Social Movements in Western Europe*. Minneapolis: University of Minnesota Press.

Lamphere, Louise. 1993. *Sunbelt Working Mothers: Reconciling Factory and Family*. Ithaca, N.Y.: Cornell University Press.

Levine, Daniel H. 1986. *Religion and Political Conflict in Latin America*. Chapel Hill: University of North Carolina Press.

Longauex y Vásquez, Enriqueta. n.d. The Woman of La Raza. Mecha Archives, box 4, no. 16. University of Texas, El Paso.

Lozano, Itziar. 1994. La Red entre Mujeres: Proyecto, avances, dificultades y propuestas. Paper presented at CEMES Conference, Chiapas, Mexico, June.

Ludec, Nathalie. 2006. La Boletina de Morelia: órgano informativo de la Red Nacional de Mujeres 1982–1985. *Comunicación y Sociedad* 5: 89–113.

Marchand, Marianne H. 2004. Neoliberal Disciplining, Violence and Transnational Organizing: The Struggle for Women's Rights in Ciudad Juárez. *Development* 47(1): 88–93.

Martínez Fernandez, Alicia Ines. 1991. *Organizaciones E Instituciones De Género*. Mexico City: FLACSO.

McAdam, Doug, and David A. Snow, eds. 1997. *Social Movements: Readings on Their Emergence, Mobilization, and Dynamics*. Los Angeles: Roxbury Publishing.

Medina, Lara. 2004. *Las Hermanas: Chicana/Latina Religious-Political Activism in the U.S. Catholic Church*. Philadelphia: Temple University Press.

Melucci, Alberto. 1995. The Process of Collective Identity. In *Social Movements and Culture*, ed. Hank Johnston and Bert Klandermans, 41–63. Minneapolis: University of Minnesota Press.

Minutes of the Michoacán General Assembly Meeting. 1995. Pátzcuaro, Michoacán: Informe y evaluación de ONGs de mujeres en Michoacán, June 24. EMAS archives.

Minutes of the Second Women's NGO Conference in Michoacán. 1994. Morelia, Michoacán, May 30. EMAS archives.

Mirandé, Alfredo, and Evangelina Enríquez. 1979. *La Chicana: The Mexican-American Woman*. Chicago: University of Chicago Press.

Moghadam, Valentine M. 2000. Transnational Feminist Networks: Collective Action in an Era of Globalization. *International Sociology* 15(1): 57–85.

Mohanty, Chandra Talpade. 2003. *Feminism without Borders: Decolonizing Theory, Practicing Solidarity*. Durham: Duke University Press.

Molina, Papusa. 1990. Recognizing, Accepting, and Celebrating Our Differences. In *Making Face, Making Soul/Haciendo Caras*, ed. Gloria Anzaldúa, 326–31. San Francisco: Aunt Lute Foundation.

Montes, Ofelia. 1987. El comedor popular: De la gestión individual a la participación colectiva. In *Estrategias de vida en el sector urbano popular*, ed. Roelfien Haak and Javier Diaz Albertini, 75–94. Lima: DESCO.

Naples, Nancy A. 1998. Women's Community Activism: Exploring the Dynamics of

Politicization and Diversity. In *Community Activism and Feminist Politics: Organizing across Race, Class, and Gender*, ed. Nancy A. Naples, 327–49. New York and London: Routledge.

Navarro, Sharon A. 2002. Las Voces de Esperanza / Voices of Hope: La Mujer Obrera, Transnationalism, and NAFTA — Displaced Women Workers in the U.S.-Mexico Borderlands. In *Globalization on the Line: Culture, Capital, and Citizenship at U.S. Borders*, ed. Claudia Sadowski-Smith, 183–200. New York: Palgrave.

Oxfam NOVIB. 2002. General Image of NOVIB. www.novib.nl/, _ Bron: _ NOVIB, _ 2002–8. Accessed August 14, 2002.

Padgett, Tim, and Cathy Booth Thomas. Two Countries, One City. *Time Magazine*, June 11, 2001.

Pardo, Mary S. 1998a. *Mexican American Women Activists: Identity and Resistance in Two Los Angeles Communities*. Philadelphia: Temple University Press.

———. 1998b. Creating Community: Mexican American Women in Eastside Los Angeles. In *Community Activism and Feminist Politics: Organizing across Race, Class, and Gender*, ed. Nancy A. Naples, 275–300. New York: Routledge.

Peña, Milagros. 1995a. Feminist Christian Women in Latin America: Other Voices, Other Visions. *Journal of Feminist Studies in Religion* 11(1): 81–94.

———. 1995b. *Theologies and Liberation in Peru: The Role of Ideas in Social Movements*. Philadelphia: Temple University Press.

———. 1996. Beijing '95 and the Women's Movement in Michoacán, Mexico: Centering Discussions on Gender, Class, and Race. *Race, Gender, and Class* 3(3): 77–87.

Reinharz, Shulamit. 1992. *Feminist Methods in Social Science Research*. New York and Oxford: Oxford University Press.

Reporte del Encuentro Feminista Latino Americano y del Caribe. 1984. *ISIS International* (June) 1:153.

Rodríguez, Lilia. 1994. Barrio Women: Between the Urban and Feminist Movement. *Latin American Perspectives* 21 (3): 32–48.

Rubén, Raúl, Evert Visser, Cor Wattel, and Jan P. de Groot. 1991. Contribución Europea al Desarrollo Democrático de las Economías Centroamericanas. In *Más Allá del Ajuste*, eds. Raúl Rubén and Govert Van Oord, 17–72. San José, Costa Rica: DEI.

Ruiz, Vicki L. 1987. By the Day or the Week: Mexicana Domestic Workers in El Paso. In *Women on the U.S.-Mexico Border: Responses to Change*, ed. Vicki L. Ruiz and Susan Tiano, 61–76. Boston: Allen and Unwin.

Sadowski-Smith, Claudia. 2002. Introduction to *Globalization on the Line: Culture, Capital, and Citizenship at U.S. Borders*, ed. Claudia Sadowski-Smith, 1–27. New York: Palgrave.

Sandoval, Chela. 1990. Feminism and Racism: A Report on the 1981 National Women's Studies Association Conference. In *Making Face, Making Soul/Haciendo Caras*, ed. Gloria Anzaldúa, 55–71. San Francisco: Aunt Lute Foundation.

Sassen, Saskia. 1998. *Globalization and Its Discontents*. New York: New Press.

Segundo Encuentro Estatal de Mujeres de Chihuahua. 1999. Optando por la Vida y Fortaleciendo la Esperanza, Cuidad Juárez, Chihuahua, 5 al 7 de Marzo.

Segura, Denise A. 1991. Ambivalence or Continuity? Motherhood and Employment among Chicanas and Mexican Immigrant Women Workers. *Aztlán* 20. 119–50.

Silva Gotay, Samuel. 1981. *El pensamiento cristiano revolucionario en América Latina*. Salamanca, Spain: Sígueme.

Simcox, David. 1993. Immigration, Population, and Economic Growth in El Paso, Texas: The Making of an American Maquiladora. *CIS Paper Series*, no. 7 (September): 1–35.

Staudt, Kathleen. 1997. Preface to *Women, International Development, and Politics: The Bureaucratic Mire*, ed. Kathleen Staudt, vii–ix. Philadelphia: Temple University Press.

Staudt, Kathleen, and Irasema Coronado. 2002. *Fronteras No Más: Toward Social Justice at the U.S.-Mexico Border*. New York: Palgrave Macmillan.

Tabuenca Córdoba, María Socorro. 1995–96. Viewing the Border: Perspectives from the Open Wound. *Discourse* 18(1–2): 146–68.

Talamante Díaz, Cecilia, Gloria Careaga Pérez, and Lorenia Parada Ampudia. 1994. Es la cooperación para las mujeres. In *Las mujeres en la pobreza*, ed. Grupo Interdisciplinario Sobre Mujer, Trabajo y Pobreza, 325–43. Mexico City: GimTrap/ Colegio de México.

Tamez, Elsa, ed. 1989. *Through Her Eyes: Women's Theology from Latin America*. New York: Orbis.

Taylor, Verta, and Nancy Whittier. 1992. Collective Identity in Social Movement Communities: Lesbian Feminist Mobilization. In *Frontiers of Social Movement Theory*, ed. Aldon D. Morris and Carol McClurg Mueller, 104–29. New Haven: Yale University Press.

Tong, Rosemarie Putnam. 1998. *Feminist Thought: A More Comprehensive Introduction*. Boulder, Colo.: Westview Press.

Trapasso, Rosa Dominga. 1990. Mujer y religión. Paper presented at Fifth Encuentro Feminista Latinoamericano y del Caribe, San Bernardo, Argentina.

United Nations. 2002. *Women Go Global*. New York: United Nations.

U.S. Census Bureau. 2000. txsdc.utsa.edu/data/census/2000/dp2_4/pdf/05048 141.pdf. Accessed June 6, 2005.

U.S. Census Bureau. 2004. Annual Social and Economic Supplement, Current Population Survey. www.bls.census.gov/cps/asec/2004/sdata.htm. Accessed July 28, 2005.

Velázquez, Margarita. 1992. *Políticas sociales, transformación agragria y participación de las mujeres en el campo, 1920–1988*. Cuernavaca, Morelos: Centro Regional de Investigaciones Multidiciplinarias, UNAM.

Vila, Pablo. 2000. *Crossing Borders, Reinforcing Borders: Social Categories, Metaphors, and Narrative Identities on the U.S.-Mexico Frontier*. Austin: University of Texas Press.

Wright, Melissa W. 1999. The Dialectics of Still Life: Murder, Women, and Maquiladoras. *Public Culture* 11(3): 453–74.

Zald, Mayer. 1992. Looking Backward to Look Forward: Reflections on the Past and Future of the Resource Mobilization Research Program. In *Frontiers in Social Movement Theory*, ed. Aldon D. Morris and Carol McClurg Mueller, 326–48. New Haven: Yale University Press.

Zavella, Patricia. 1987. *Women's Work and Chicano Families: Cannery Workers of the Santa Clara Valley*. Ithaca, N.Y.: Cornell University Press.

———. 1997. Reflections on Diversity among Chicanas. In *Challenging Fronteras: Structuring Latina and Latino Lives in the U.S.*, ed. Mary Romero, Pierrette Hondagneu-Sotelo, and Vilma Ortiz, 187–94. New York: Routledge.

Index

ference on Women and, 103–7; faith-based organizations in, 125–33; future of NGOs in, 147–52; grass-roots networking in, 14–21; health and education issues for women in, 87–95; history and geography of, 72–74; homelessness in, 79–87; labor issues in, 74–79; research methodology in, 28–30; violence against women in, 87–97; women's activism in, 2–6, 29–30, 70–107

civil associations, 139–41

class-based politics: in El Paso/Ciudad Juárez, 14–21, 23–24; grassroots activism and, 2, 10, 13, 154n.3; health initiatives in Michoacán and, 55–60

coalition and collaboration: conflict and competition as result of, 141–45; of El Paso/Ciudad Juárez activists, 82–87, 90–95; in Latina/o communities, 20–21, 24–26; limits to feminist politics of, 3

Cohen, Jean L., 131

Colectivo de Lucha contra la Violencia hacia las Mujeres, A. C. (COVAC; Fight against Violence toward Women Collective, Inc.), 12

Collins, Patricia Hill, 85

Colonias Development Council of Doña Ana County, New Mexico, 29

colonias populares (Mexico), 33

Color Purple, The, 85

Comandante Ramona, 43

Combs, Rosemary, 95

Comisión de Mujeres (Women's Commission), 117

Comisión Evangélica Latinoamericana

de Educación Cristiana (CELADEC; Latin American Evangelical Commission for Christian Education), 138–41

community issues: AIDS initiative in Michoacán as, 56–60; indigenous activists' involvement in, 63–65; Michoacán women activists' initiatives concerning, 39–42; self-esteem and empowerment through organization of, 97–103

Comunicación, Intercambio y Desarrollo Humano en América Latina (CIDHAL; Communication, Exchange, and Human Development in Latin America), 10, 117–25, 139–43

comunidades eclesiales de base (CEBS; base Christian communities), 9–10, 154n.4

Concha, Eleanor Aida (Sister), 28, 106, 108–11, 130–33

Confederación Latinoamericana de Religiosos (CLAR; Confederation of Latin American Religious), 108–33

Conference of Major Superiors of Women, 129

Conferencia Episcopal Latinoamericana (CELAM; Latin American Bishops' Conference), 7, 27, 53–54, 109–11, 119–20

Conferencia Intercontinental de Teólogas del Tercer Mundo, 117

Conferencia Latinoamericana de Iglesias (CLAI; Latin American Council of Churches), 122

Consejo Nacional de Población (CONAPO; National Population Council), 31–33

MacArthur Foundation grant to Viva Natura, 48–49

machismo, Latina confrontation with, 89

machista system and women's oppression, 23

"malinchistas," feminists derided as, 16

maquiladoras, 73–79

Martínez, Alicia, 8

Maryknoll order, feminist initiatives of, 113–15

Mejía, María Consuelo, 28

Melucci, Alberto, 19, 150

Méndez Arceo, Sergio (Bishop), 131–33

Mexican Americans: activist strategies of, 4–6; conflict with recent immigrants, 93–95; definitions of, 153n.1; growth of NGOs for, 8–9

Mexico: Beijing conference preparations by NGOs in, 11–13; earthquake of 1985 in, 34–35, 60–65; grassroots movements in El Paso/Ciudad Juárez and women in, 14–21; growth of NGOs in, 8–9; history of indigenous activism in, 61; political strategies of women activists in, 40–42; registration of NGOs in, 8; strategies of women activists in, 4–6, 31–69; women's education statistics in, 31; women's labor statistics in, 31–32; women's movement in, 9–11, 39–69

Michoacán, Mexico: ecological approaches of women activists in, 46–49; funding strategies of NGOs in, 137–41; future of NGOs in, 147–52; health initiatives of women activists in, 54–60; women activists and indigenous groups, 60–65; outreach strategies of women activists in, 42–46; political strategies of women activists in, 38–42; religious activities of women activists in, 51–54; research methodology in, 27; "Toward Beijing" efforts of NGOs in, 11–13, 67–69; women's activism in, 2–6, 29–30, 31–69

Michoacanos Unidos por la Salud y contra el Sida, A.C. (MUSSAC; Michoacanos United for Health and against AIDS, Inc.), 27, 56–60

Michoacán State Coordinating Committee, 11

Mirandé, Alfredo, 72

Moghadam, Valentine, 28, 134

Mohanty, Chandra Talpade, 23, 84, 149

Molina, Papusa, 25

Monreal Molina, Patricia, 76–79, 96–99, 102–4, 126, 141–42, 150

Montes, Ofelia, 24

Montoya, Francisca, 3–4, 105–7

Mujeres de la Conferencia Cristiana por la Paz (CCP; Women of the Christian Conference for Peace), 122–123

Mujeres del Magisterio Democrático (Women for Democratic Teaching), 27, 43–46

Mujeres de Nocutzepo, 27

Mujeres en Acción Sindical (Women for Union Action), 142–43

Mujeres Grupo Erandi de Pichátaro (Erandi Women's Group of Pichátaro), 12–13, 27, 60–66

Mujeres para el Diálogo (MPD; Women for Dialogue), 10, 27–28, 48, 104, 106–7, 109–33

Mujeres por la Democracia (Women for Democracy), 4–5, 27, 41–42, 147

Mujeres Unidas (Women United) Cooperative, 29, 102, 133

Nación Purépecha (Purépecha Nation), 12–13, 27, 60–65, 147

Naples, Nancy A., 152

Navarrette, Dolores, 104–5

Navarro, Fernanda, 36

Navarro, Sharon, 6, 23, 71

networking: by grassroots women's movements, 12–13, 49; homelessness initiatives in El Paso-Ciudad Juárez and, 83–87; Latina use of, 20–21; by Michoacán women activists, 68–69; NGOs' reliance on, 146–52; by religious feminists, 115–17, 132–33; research methodology concerning, 27

New Mexico Community Foundation, 102

New York Times, 73–74, 113–14

Nicaraguan Frente Sandinista de Liberación Nacional (Sandinista National Liberation Front), 10

nongovernmental organizations (NGOs): activist strategies of, 2–6, 153n.2; coalitions and alliances among, 25–26; conflict and competition among, 141–45; cross-border activities of, 71–107; ecological strategies in Michoacán of, 46–49; educational initiatives of, 89–95; in El Paso/Ciudad Juárez, 2–6, 14–24, 29–30, 70–107; empowerment of Latinas through, 85–87; evolution in Mexico of, 9–11; faith-based initiatives and, 127–33; feminists' role in, 16–18; funding issues for, 134–45; future of, 146–52; global capitalism and growth of, 6–9; health initiatives of,

54–60, 87–95; homeless women in El Paso and, 82–87; indigenous activists and, 60–65; Latin American feminism and, 116–17; limitations of, 3, 102–7; Mexican earthquake and role of, 34, 60–65; origins in U.S. Southwest of, 7–8; outreach strategies in Michoacán of, 42–46; religious approaches in Michoacán by, 49–50; research methodology on activism of, 26–30; self-esteem and empowerment initiatives of, 98–103; "Toward Beijing" movement in Michoacán and, 66–69

North American Free Trade Agreement (NAFTA), 7

No Turning Back, 114

NOVIB research on NGOs, 143–45

Nuestro clamor por la vida, 22

oral history methodology: on grass-roots women's movements, 26–30; Latina research using, 2

Organización Popular Independiente (OPI; Popular Independent Organization), 28–29, 76–77, 82–87, 96–103, 126, 141, 150

outreach strategies of women activists in Michoacán, 42–46

Padgett, Tim, 72

Padilla Hernán, Dolores, 35

Parada Ampudia, Lorenia, 6, 10–12, 35

Pardo, Mary, 25, 93, 97, 99

Partido de la Revolución Democrática (PRD; Party of the Democratic Revolution), 41–42

Partido Revolucionario Institucional (PRI; Institutional Revolutionary Party), 41–42, 66, 77

Milagros Peña is an associate professor of sociology and director of the Center for Women's Studies and Gender Research at the University of Florida. She is the author of *Theologies and Liberation in Peru: The Role of Ideas in Social Movements* (1995) and coauthor (with Curry Malott) of *Punk Rockers' Revolution: A Pedagogy of Race, Class and Gender* (2004). She is coeditor (with Edwin I. Hernández, Kenneth G. Davis, and Elizabeth Station) of *Emerging Voices, Urgent Choices: Essays on Latino/a Religious Leadership* (2006).

Library of Congress Cataloging-in-Publication Data

Peña, Milagros

Latina activists across borders : women's grassroots organizing

in Mexico and Texas / Milagros Peña.

p. cm.

Includes bibliographical references and index.

ISBN 978-0-8223-3936-6 (cloth : alk. paper)

ISBN 978-0-8223-3951-9 (pbk. : alk. paper)

1. Women social reformers — Mexico. 2. Women social reformers — Texas.

3. Hispanic American women — Mexico. 4. Hispanic American

women — Texas. 5. Women human rights workers — Mexico.

6. Women human rights workers — Texas.   I. Title.

HN49.W6P46 2007   305.420972'1 — dc22   2006033806